Urban Development 2120

Urban Development 2120

Peter Nelson

 BUSINESS EXPERT PRESS

First published in 2019 by
Business Expert Press, LLC
222 East 46th Street, New York, NY 10017
www.businessexpertpress.com

ISBN-13: 978-1-94999-109-3 (paperback)
ISBN-13: 978-1-94999-110-9 (e-book)

Business Expert Press Economics and Public Policy Collection

Collection ISSN: 2163-761X (print)
Collection ISSN: 2163-7628 (electronic)

Cover and interior design by S4Carlisle Publishing Services Private Ltd., Chennai, India

First edition: 2019

10 9 8 7 6 5 4 3 2 1

Printed in the United States of America.

Abstract

The year 2120 may appear a long way into the future but will come quickly. The global population reached one billion in 1804, four billion in 1974, six billion in 1999, seven billion in 2012, and nine billion predicted for 2020.

Given the speed of current development under the threat of changing climate, this book attempts to project ahead but with a particular focus.

Housing and feeding so many people is about saving the planet while laying the foundations for a quality of life that is within what people in 2120 will want in their living conditions. One factor has not been considered, namely, how each new generation comes in at a different reference point. Previously, the ideal home might have had a house, a garden, perhaps a swimming pool or tennis court. Teenagers today don't care about these amenities as long as they have access to their electronic devices. Grandparents might resent living in one-room apartments, while young people could find this acceptable. The planning conundrum is to anticipate the expectations of future generations.

This text looks at best theories of urban development, attempting to integrate future expectations in the hope of guiding governments to think outside the box.

Keywords

carbon capture; cluster development; diversity; greening; land use; planning; poverty elimination; spatial; sponge city; super city; urban design; urban development; urban planning; urbanization

JEL Classification: F35,64: G28;O018,O044,O057; R11,12,14,21,38, 51,52,58.

Contents

Acknowledgments

This book is dedicated to my daughter, Tina, who turned my attention away from how I might look at the world toward what the young people today might see as more important. If she could see such a disparity between what generations might desire, this started me thinking about how things might be played out 100 years from now, taking into account accelerating technology incomprehensible in the not too distant past. Would she, her children, and grandchildren still want open spaces to run around in, or would they feel more comfortable connected to their devices and become self-sufficient within some electronic cocoon? Her prompting this line of thinking filled me with dread at such prospects but eventually led me to the conclusion that each new generation enters from a level of personal perspective and they, like so many before us, are likely to adjust and still survive.

Introduction

Projections of a global population approaching the nine-billion mark make it reasonable to expect that the planet will come under increasing stress and so too its ability to host an environment that is livable and sustainable for the entire human race. With connectivity between people of different ethnic origins and values having to share limited space, governments will need to be able to define the most favorable parameters within which people can live and carry out their daily functions while at the same time enjoying a conducive environment in safety.

The global population is believed to have reached the first billion mark in 1804, 4 billion in 1974, 6 billion in 1999, 7 billion in 2012, is close to the 9 billion predicted for 2020, and heading for 15 billion projected for 2120.[1] Dramatic changes are therefore in the offing, not just in definable stages, as in the past, but through quantum leaps through new technology, connectivity between people, and the fight for limited global resources as humans need to find their own space and identity.

Within this population projection, cities to which populations are migrating are believed to generate 70 percent of the world's GDP and account for over 60 percent of global energy consumption, while generating 70 percent of global greenhouse gas emissions as well as 70 percent of global solid waste.[2] As clusters of population concentrate in urban regions, cities and towns are likely to become even more vulnerable to natural disasters and impacts of climate change, but this is the point toward which people are moving.

Housing the future population will need careful planning and considerable finance. With the rapid development of technology and the emergence of artificial intelligence replacing many jobs, systems will need to be created to handle the changing employment landscape, from the traditional nine-to-five workday and from holding one type of job for life. Considerable social engineering will take place, and the planners will need

[1]United Nations. 2014. *World Urbanization Prospects: The 2014 Revision* (New York, NY: United Nations Population Division).
[2]See: http://habitat3.org/the-new-urban-agenda

to preempt these changes to offer the greening spaces society can look forward to. An important issue will be this: Who will emerge as the global decision makers, and, in the end, will the population accept their decisions?

Forward projections will not be easy for planners to make within global development goals where the integration between the very poor living in slums and those financially better off who want to maintain their lifestyles will be thwarted by severe conflicts. Planning will need to be able to reduce potential tensions between different classes of society, creating the necessity of providing living spaces and interconnectivity while somehow maintaining the quality of life.

The operative word here is "connectivity," since all of these planning activities have to be linked and none of them are mutually exclusive. Therefore, first, it is necessary to lay out all the relevant data and then work toward connecting the dots. That is what the following pages seek to do, beginning with an attempt to identify the overall problem. It is inevitable that very many things will change during the next 100 years, and the level and nature of changes will depend on the current state of development in various countries; thus, it is impossible to find a one-size-fits-all solution. Particularly relevant, as demonstrated in the past, are those quantum leap inventions such as fire, the wheel, electricity, the telephone, and the Internet, each bringing with them linkages to aligned development. Consequently, it is not possible to forecast interconnecting influences, so in the following text components constituting urban development are provided as a checklist indicating how they are likely to develop and thus attempting to provide a blueprint for how they will all fit together.

As countries face the looming challenges, it is clear that many lack robust national urban policies or strategies to tackle the needs of a rapidly growing urban population and that their weak urban planning systems are unable to respond to those challenges. Nevertheless, from an overall perspective, the following three global agendas underline the importance of public policy and action oriented toward sustainable and resilient urban development:

- The New Urban Agenda,[3] adopted at the United Nations Conference on Housing and Sustainable Urban Development (Habitat III), held

---

[3]United Nations. 2017. *The New Urban Agenda, A/RES/71/256*. Habitat III and United Nations.

in October 2016 in Quito, Ecuador, highlights numerous challenges that cities face: poor housing, need for improved urban resilience and disaster risk reduction plans, and inadequate provision of urban infrastructure and services, including water supply and sanitation and urban mobility and public transport. For the implementation of the New Urban Agenda, UN-Habitat has proposed action targeting five areas: (i) national urban policies; (ii) urban legislation, rules and regulations; (iii) urban planning and design; (iv) urban economy and municipal finance; and (v) local implementation.[4]

- The Paris Agreement invites cities, as nonparty stakeholders, "to scale up their efforts and support actions to reduce emissions and/or to build resilience and decrease vulnerability to the adverse effects of climate change."[5]
- The Sendai Framework for Disaster Risk Reduction, 2015 to 2030, has established the following goal: "Prevent new and reduce existing disaster risk through the implementation of integrated and inclusive economic, structural, legal, social, health, cultural, educational, environmental, technological, political and institutional measures that prevent and reduce hazard exposure and vulnerability to disaster, increase preparedness for response and recovery, and thus strengthen resilience."[6]

Some global changes have initiated these perspectives. One is the focus on countries with massive populations and their growth, for example, China and India, with the recognition that some of these areas are particularly vulnerable. Highlighting this is the fact that between 1950 and 2014, Southeast Asia experienced rapid urbanization, with more than 1,000 percent urban growth.[7] "Southeast Asian cities are highly vulnerable to the impacts of climate change and natural disasters given their

[4]UN-Habitat. 2017. *Action Framework for Implementation of the New Urban Agenda* (Nairobi, Kenya: UN-Habitat).

[5]United Nations. 2015. "Adoption of the Paris Agreement, Resolution FCCC/ CP/2015/L.9/Rev.1." https://unfccc.int/resource/docs/2015/cop21/eng/l09r01.pdf

[6]United Nations. 2015. *Sendai Framework for Disaster Risk Reduction, 2015–2030* (New York, NY: United Nations).

[7]D. Bharat. 2014. "Southeast Asia and Sustainable Urbanization," *Global Asia* 9, no. 3, pp. 84–91.

unique geographies and high population densities. The result is that most cities find themselves perpetually in fire-fighting mode."[8] The region is also witnessing a "staggering expansion of a 'consuming class' that will spur demand for private vehicles and, in turn, create an enormous increase in greenhouse gas emissions, with the potential of further exacerbating climate change and its worldwide impacts."[9]

Most countries agree that the problem needs to be addressed, but beyond recognizing the issue have reached no overall agreement on how the objectives can be met.

In addition, after looking at all of the plans and concepts for the future, this is being done from the present-day perspective. The real question is, what sort of human will evolve under the constraints of living in inevitably close proximity? Will they revolt in some way, and what would be the outcome of that; or will they simply accept what they are told and, with their new technology assistance and robotics, drift more into themselves and think everything is fine?

There is always a danger in making predictions when everything is put into one box, as there is always natural progression. The answer in defining an issue is to first define all the facts and let them point the way to an outcome. That is what is attempted here.

It is hard to know whether what current planners think future generations will want will turn out to be accurate or even nearly accurate. Perhaps people coming onto the planet in 100 years will want a totally different way of living and be perfectly happy with different services. Reported evidence shows that in developing countries the 10- to 20-year-old demographic obtain their news from bites off their devices but demonstrate no political interest otherwise.[10] That group may be happy to live in a cocoon-style accommodation or may have ambitions of living on Mars. For now, all that planners can do is make assumptions and hope they get most of them right.

---

[8]Ibid. p. 88.

[9]D. Bharat. 2016. "ASEAN Economic Integration and Sustainable Urbanization," *Journal of Urban Culture Research* 12, pp. 8–14. doi: 10.14456/jucr.2016.10

[10]Radio Station 2GB Australia, Knights with Steve Price and Andrew Bolt, November 1, 2018.

CHAPTER 1

Predicting the Future

Humans emerged from their caves or climbed down from the trees to first wander the earth, living on hunting, then went on to "slash and burn" before planting crops and settling down in habitats. Over centuries, there were major leaps forward with inventions such as fire and the wheel. Later, eyeglasses were invented, allowing science to look at and design the small, while telescopes explored the heavens. Cities were formed while eyes still looked to the stars. Just over a 100 years ago man took to flight, and in July 1969, men landed on the moon. Today, they are planning to populate Mars.

Coupled with projected earthly population growth which will have people living in closer proximity, this in itself will necessitate major changes, as will the interconnectivity between humans, allowing governments to trace all movements and anticipate everyone's requirements giving them full control.

What is known for certain? Only a little. But there will be more people needing to somehow make a living, meaning they will still need access to food and shelter and somehow pay for that. Currency was in primitive form based on acquiring and exchanging of shells, before people graduated to offering promissory notes that governments later turned into currency promises. This paper, or currency, was originally backed by gold, but that became too limiting, so it was decided that people just had to trust government.[1] The next move will be into cyber-currency of some kind, again backed by government and its ability to pay.

---

[1]While paper money was originally backed by gold held, it was manipulated over a long time until it could no longer be supported, and the gold standard was abandoned with other currencies pegged now against U.S. dollars held as reserve currency, not gold. The EU want the Euro as another pegging standard, as does China with the RMB.

Obviously, there are no difficulties if governments can be counted on to meet their debts but with mounting deficits in, say, the United States, the question becomes whether this is sustainable or whether in geopolitical terms the debt becomes part of an international contest.[2] Each of these issues raises more questions than definitive answers but needs to be raised anyway.

The elephant in the room is, considering that if an overwhelming population can no longer be supported by available resources, will human engineering kick in to determine who lives and who dies, and of course, more importantly, who makes that decision?

What are the unknowns? Unknowns are all of the contributing factors discussed, but one way or the other, people will still need somewhere to live on earth, and until "living" also means the possibility of doing so on another planet, people would still need to be living in close proximity: an urban environment. So what will that be in 2120 and will those future inhabitants want to design it differently?

---

[2]Whereas the United States runs continuing and mounting deficits, in China the balance of payments recorded a surplus of US$ 257.9 billion in 2014; so the United States is running massive deficits, while China can maintain surpluses and also hold the largest portion of U.S. foreign debt.

CHAPTER 2

Greening and Global Warming Response

Importance

Much has been said of climate change since it is an emotive banner headline, but the term should be better defined since climate has always been changing. The current hypothesis is that it is changing because of man-made global warming and something needs to be done about it. Unfortunately, for the way the subject is presented, it detracts from the real need to address some serious environmental issues.

Overall, there is a need to look at planet Earth as a limited environment having to cater to an ever-expanding population that will soon approach nine billion. If there is global warming with a detrimental impact on the planet and if part of the global warming is man-made and hence mitigable, the problem needs to be discussed and a rational solution devised on a bipartisan basis instead of using it as the political and socioeconomic football that it has become over the past three decades. On the one hand, there are well-meaning people looking simplistically at how warming can be reversed (as Australia not wanting to use their own cheap coal), while on the other is a group deriving political mileage from this, gathering voter support and building their economies by going ahead and using coal and nuclear energy (supplied by Australia to China, India, Japan, etc.) for their population's energy needs.

Eventually, cost–benefit analysis will determine the outcomes and resolve how power will be generated, and hopefully, logic rather than emotion will prevail. The bottom line here is that there are two alternatives for 2120: power will either be available to all or need to be rationed in some way, since although electric cars may reduce emission levels, the electricity has to be manufactured initially. Otherwise, apart from solar panels and wind turbines to overcome low availability, projects such as Australia's "Snowy 2" are under way, in which water will be pumped uphill when there is power and used for hydro generation when there is no power. Other new methods too will become available.

It is hard to envisage a global economy giving up on electricity supply after having developed this far, but then the State of South Australia did run out of electricity and had to "borrow" coal fired generated electricity from Victoria in 2017 when its wind farms had to be shut down for lack of wind.

Overall the problems with use of "green energy" are not so much about how to create it but rather about how to store it. In future batteries will be improved and this will have enormous effects on methods of power generation. This, then, is an entirely cost–benefit issue at the center of the current debate.

Aims in Greening

In addressing greening and global warming, the major aim should be to allow the planet to remain in the best possible condition for all forms of life and continue to the best of its ability. This is a very broad objective but it underscores the importance of greening for humans, as it is now known how significantly plant life reduces residual carbon emissions and therefore how important it is to save the trees. That the conservation concept is by no means new is reflected by one of the earliest quoted references to green planning that appears to have been made around AD 650, when Caliph Abu Bakr commanded his army not to harm trees. Otherwise, the main aim is to promote *green* and *resilient* cities.

Environmental sustainability is fundamental to ensuring the prosperity and well-being of all people within planetary boundaries, including the promotion of prosperous and innovative cities with a particular focus on growth and job creation. This is within the scope of promoting good urban governance by strengthening the capacity of the authorities at all levels of government in integrated planning and public finance management, by establishing adequate legal and policy frameworks, by fostering access to public and private investments by municipalities, and by supporting women's empowerment in urban governance matters. These are all admirable aspirations but need to be incorporated into future plans.

Climate Change

Climate has changed throughout the Earth's history; where in the past 650,000 years, there have been seven cycles of glacial advance and retreat. The end of the last ice age, about 7,000 years ago, marked the beginning of the modern climate era.

Most of the change has something to do with the slight shift of the Earth to the sun, over which humans have little control, raising the question, what is the human contribution to warming, and, if this is in fact detrimental, does the warming need to be arrested, and if so from a planning perspective what should be done about it through what kinds of measures?

So first let's ask whether there is global warming. The general consensus among experts on this question is that there is a 95 percent probability that global warming is occurring and that the rise has been unprecedented through the mid-20th century.[1] Similar postulates are based on the judgment that greenhouse gases are the main contributing factor to the increased rate of warming through heat-trapping carbon dioxide (CO_2) and other gases. It is estimated how the planet's average surface temperature has risen about 1.62°F (0.9°C) since the late 19th century, a change

---

[1] IPCC Fifth Assessment Report, Summary for Policymakers: B.D. Santer, K.E. Taylor, T.M.L. Wigley, et al. July 4, 1996. "A Search for Human Influences on the Thermal Structure of the Atmosphere," *Nature* 382, pp. 39–46; G.C. Hegerl, H. Storch, and K. Hasselmann. October 1996. "Detecting Greenhouse-Gas-Induced Climate Change with an Optimal Fingerprint Method," *Journal of Climate* 9, pp. 2281–306; V. Ramaswamy, M.D. Schwarzkopf, W.J. Randel, B.D. Santer, B.J. Soden, and G.L. Stenchikov. February 24, 2006. "Anthropogenic and Natural Influences in the Evolution of Lower Stratospheric Cooling," *Science* 311, pp. 1138–141; B.D. Santer, M.F. Wehner, T.M.L. Wigley, R. Sausen, G.A. Meehl, K.E. Taylor, C. Ammann, J. Arblaster, W.M. Washington, J.S. Boyle, and W. Brüggemann. July 25, 2003. "Contributions of Anthropogenic and Natural Forcing to Recent Tropopause Height Changes," *Science* 301, pp. 479–83.

driven largely by increased CO_2 and other human-made emissions into the atmosphere.[2]

It is also reported that 2016 was the warmest year on record, since records were kept and general trends show that general warming and changing weather patterns do in fact exist. In addition, oceans have been absorbing much of this increased heat, with the top 700 meters (about 2,300 feet) of ocean showing a temperature increase of 0.302°F since 1969.[3] Also recorded are shrinking ice sheets, glacial retreats, decreased snow cover, sea level rise, declining Arctic Sea ice, and ocean acidification. Most of the latter details are really not in dispute, while the extent of human contribution is a subject of controversy.

Unfortunately, while obviously unprecedented excessive global warming is a matter of concern, historical political expedience seems to have introduced multi-issue social engineering and to have distorted the issue when it should receive serious bipartisan analysis. For example, the much promoted Paris Agreement starts by saying that signatories must "respect," promote, and consider their respective obligations on human rights, the right to health, the right of indigenous peoples, local communities, migrants, children, persons with disabilities and people in vulnerable situations, and the right to development, as well as gender equality, empowerment of women, and intergenerational equity. It also includes a reference to "climate justice," whatever that means, along with the need for "eradicating poverty." Neither does it help to focus on rational argument and support when the UN Intergovernmental Panel on Climate Change (IPCC) announced in 2018 that we have only 12 years left to save the planet.[4] This, after Al Gore's 2006 movie, *An inconvenient truth*, only gave the planet until 2016. Again, the problem is that predictions of calamities make for ridiculous assertions, including one proclaiming that to save the planet people should, among other measures, stop eating meat so as to prevent cows from emitting methane. This makes the

---

[2]National Center for environmental Information.

[3]S. Levitus, J.I. Antonov, T.P. Boyer, R.A. Locarnini, H.E. Garcia, and A.V. Mishonov. 2009. "Global Ocean Heat Content 1955–2008 in Light of Recently Revealed Instrumentation Problems," *Geophysical Research Letters* 36, no. 7.

[4]IPCC announcement October 8, 2018.

issue comical when it should be treated seriously. Equally farcical is the fact that the United States and China, the biggest polluters, are not even signatories to the Paris Agreement, again while everyone should at least be taking the issue seriously.

Thus, the consensus is that climate is changing, but whether humans have contributed or not remains an issue to be taken seriously and calls for meticulous planning with a view to providing for a sustainable earthly habitat 100 years from now.

Reduction of Carbon Emissions

If, as it is argued, carbon emissions contribute to the planet's global warming, and that is a bad thing, a major part of the planning process for urban development has to be reduction of carbon emissions. The other part of the equation is in designing future urban habitats that can respond to normal human aspirations while at the same time preventing unpleasant consequences brought about by the changing climate. Of these, the perceived major factors would be increased temperatures; extreme weather conditions; rising sea levels bringing about flooding; changes in cultivation, crops, and livestock; and depletion of fish stocks.[5] The bottom line seems to be "can humans stop global warming?" and "if they can't stop global warming, at least plan to live with it."

The main issue in regard to reducing carbon emissions is whether the cost can be reduced, the cost of achieving various percentages of reduction, the cost of partial reduction and, in reality, how much of the problem humans can still live with against percentage reduction.

To start addressing these questions, one needs to identify the major polluters and the components of their pollution. Those identified as targets in this area include the coal-burning power-generating plants and factories releasing emissions. On the local level, there are high emissions from vehicles that since Henry Ford's model Ford, in 1923 (costing $300), have given populations mobility, which they are reluctant to relinquish, even though sitting in traffic jams wasn't what the original car

---

[5]Ocean shock report, Reuters, showing schools of fish moving owing to rising sea temperature, November 2018.

promised. On a global basis, there is also a glaring contradiction: where on the one hand, governments are making serious efforts to curtail private cars and encourage consumers to switch to hybrids while, on the other, in developing countries the number of vehicles being added to the roads is increasing rapidly. If people do not wish to forgo their polluting pleasures, governments will eventually be forced to adopt the "user-pays" model, as Singapore did in a pioneering move, introducing a fee for entering built-up areas and a subsequent charge for use per mile.[6] While in the past such systems have been difficult to monitor and implement, the use of current technology would make it less difficult to tag vehicles and bill them for the use of any public roads. Such a system also overcomes the fact that while government can tax petrol they miss out on revenue from electric vehicles.

Power-generating emissions or polluting companies can be monitored and controlled by governments; thus, if the population still demands power and factories want power, in order to earn income, both can be taxed. The cost–benefit consideration comes again into play, inevitably bringing with it a political dimension.

This debate on levels of carbon reduction is driven largely by political expediency. To mark its 50th anniversary celebrations, China had to clear the almost unbreathable smog from the air in Beijing and did so by simply ordering polluting enterprises to relocate. On the other hand, in Australia, which has the world's largest supply of usable coal and uranium, politicians have realized the opportunity for a "green" vote and thus do not allow those resources to form part of long-term plans; yet they allow export of those resources to major polluters in order to drive their economy, and this merely shifts the problem from one country to others.

In order to supplant coal-fired power generation, which is still the cheapest method of generating electricity beyond hydropower, alternative methods such as wind turbines and solar panels need to be subsidized by governments since they are more expensive per unit of power than coal, while nuclear power stations bring with them emotive connotations.

---

[6]Other methods include Greece's rule of allowing cars with different number plates on the roads on different days; this did not work too well as people bought junk cars for the plates.

In relation to pollution from motor vehicles, electric propulsion eliminates carbon emissions on the road but there remains the need to generate electricity to charge the batteries in the vehicles in the first place. This power question seems to be heavily centered on storage and quality of batteries, since production is limited when the wind doesn't blow and the sun doesn't shine.

Overall, an attitude of hypocrisy pervades the issue, as reflected by some developed countries being out of touch with reality, trying to feel good about reducing emissions, while other countries pollute away with abandon.[7]

The issue returns to one where there is a need for a global approach, which has not yet emerged because of political systems and the concern with looking after one's own local population. The view 100 years from now projects the need to move toward a more centralized control of the planet to overcome the conflicting carbon reduction policies. What however usually comes with such authoritarianism is not always appreciated.

Carbon Credit Funding

Irrespective of the concept of global warming and its possible wider ramifications, planning needs to promote the social dimensions of sustainable urban development through inclusive and safe cities. Inclusiveness is the fight against urban poverty and exclusion.

To deal with the first part of the equation—"can global warming be stopped?"—the likely answer is no, but perhaps it can be slowed down, given the possible consequences. If carbon is a strong contributor to global warming, as with most things on the planet, a possible remedy is to attach a cost–benefit tag to it. One way to reduce carbon emissions is by creating "carbon credits"[8] around polluters. This can be done by allowing "cash" credits for activities that reduce carbon emissions, which can be offset against other polluting factors, traded or redeemed for cash.

---

[7]For example, in the Philippines over 200 vehicles were documented, in November 2018, as parked with drivers in a car park running the engines for their air conditioners. In many developed countries, it is illegal to hang clothing to dry on balconies, so people are forced to use expensive energy-consuming clothes driers.

[8]One carbon credit is equivalent to one ton of CO_2 emissions.

Once created, the carbon credits can be swapped between polluters, lowering their "carbon footprint," or traded on a carbon market.

The main limitation of this concept is that not everyone is on the same playing field, obviously because the largest polluters are not really penalized for nonaction. This is where certain polluters pay the pollution penalty and simply pass the cost on to the consumer. On the other hand, it does bring in the cost–benefit or user-pays concept, thereby recognizing the problem as being one of encouraging companies to adopt emission-reducing methods if it is in their financial interest to do so or face pressure from the governments to develop and execute plans to reduce emissions.

China, to cite specific case, enjoys a low cost of production, particularly in regard to labor and power. To maintain its domestic production, it will steer clear of introducing policies that will raise the cost of either of these, and will instead keep using pollutants if necessary. There being no effective way to prevent rising pollution costs, absent government policy to the contrary, polluters will continue to pollute. The limiting factor is when governments become embarrassed by obvious and unsightly pollution, which, however, the Chinese government will be able to keep under the radar.[9]

Nevertheless, there are various carbon credit funds, a notable case being that of the EU, which takes this question seriously. There are also mutual funds and other financial vehicles that aim to move in this direction. The latest development has been the proposed introduction of a cryptocurrency carbon trading platform, which, though not a major initiative at present while the world is trying to adjust to the cryptocurrency model, does signal a direction for the future where individuals and not just companies, could become involved.

Global Coordinated Action

Considering that all humans are on the same planet and there will be increasing interface between populations in different countries, there is a

---

[9]International news agencies accredited to China are required to have official approval for any stories they file.

need for coordinated global action rather than mere rhetoric in relation to environmental sustainability issues.

On the one hand, the Scandinavian countries have had a plastic and bottle recycling policy for more than 20 years and take their environmental issues seriously, whereas in some other countries not even lip service is paid to addressing environmental issues. Neither do long-term benefits accrue from the attempts of one country with a contribution to greenhouse gas emissions of less than 2 percent to contain its emissions further, while major polluters carry on with little restraint.[10]

A global response led by the UN resulted in the Kyoto protocol followed by the Paris Agreement, leading to further studies. On October 6, 2018, IPCC released a special report on the impacts of global warming that indicated a 1.5°C temperature rise above preindustrial levels and highlighted related global greenhouse gas emission pathways, in the context of strengthening the global response to the threat of climate change, sustainable development, and poverty eradication.[11]

The report headlines at its paragraph A2.2.,that "Reaching and sustaining 'net-zero global anthropogenic CO_2 emissions' and declining net non-CO_2 radiative forcing 'would halt anthropogenic global warming on multi-decadal timescales (high confidence).' The maximum temperature reached is then determined by cumulative net global anthropogenic CO_2 emissions up to the time of net-zero CO_2 emissions (high confidence) and the level of non-CO_2 radiative forcing in the decades prior to the time that maximum temperatures are reached (medium confidence). On longer timescales, sustained net negative global anthropogenic CO_2 emissions and/or further reductions in non-CO_2 radiative forcing may still be required to prevent further warming due to Earth system feedbacks and reverse ocean acidification (medium confidence) and will be required to minimize sea level rise (high confidence)." (Cross-Chapter Box 2 in Chapter 1, 1.2.3, 1.2.4, Figure 1.4, 2.2.1, 2.2.2, 3.4.4.8, 3.4.5.1, 3.6.3.2)

---

[10] Australia, *The Guardian*, August 2017.

[11] This summary for policymakers was formally approved at the First Joint Session of Working Groups I, II, and III of the IPCC and accepted by the 48th Session of the IPCC, Incheon, Republic of Korea, October 6, 2018. http://report.ipcc.ch/sr15/pdf/sr15_spm_final.pdf

While the report is well meaning and reassuring, in that so many experts are addressing the issue, and contains an abundance of statistical evidence, it does not resolve any conflicting issues immediately but raises them all over again by stating that reaching **net-zero global anthropogenic CO$_2$ emissions** would **halt anthropogenic global warming.** The general public would focus on this one statement as the definitive argument to stop all emissions, ignoring the fact that the planet is warming anyway and that the issue is not this but man's contribution.

Hence, the question of agreeing on a global action plan is important, but attempts such as the Paris Accord and the reports as previously detailed have failed to achieve this objective. A simple solution does not exist, but the approach to one lies in the realm of economics. Wealthy societies can pay to be environmentally "friendly," while for countries with large poor populations it is more difficult. Education is one thing but try and explain that to someone living on the street. Action has to be backed by government-led policies aligned to "user pays" with subsidy to cover those incapable of paying. This would constitute a meaningful urban design concept.

CHAPTER 3

Population Expansion

Global

The defining figures that depict global urban settlements follow predictions on global human population growth at 83 million annually, or 1.1 percent per year.[1] The global population, which was at 7.616 billion in 2018, is estimated to reach 8.6 billion by mid-2030, 9.8 billion by mid-2050, and at least 11.2 billion by 2100, an increase of about 32 percent. The figures indicate that a great deal will obviously have to change in most ways people live their lives and how they will be controlled.

A major factor is that many nations with rapid population growth have low standards of living (Africa has the highest projected population growth), whereas many nations with low rates of population growth have high standards of living, raising the question whether this trend will continue in the long run and whether populations will live comfortably with the change.

Migration

Human migration has taken place since man first climbed out of the cave or had to move because of the lack of trees. With the survival gene built into humanity, as with all animals, the search for new sources of food and refuge from danger has been relentless. While it might be an uncomfortable concept, the reality is that humans are an advanced form of animal in the evolutionary chain and hence, although it is postulated that conflict between ethnic and tribal divisions as well as between religions can be curtailed or mitigated, it is more likely that conflict between such groups

---

[1] UN World Population Prospects 2017.

will continue, particularly as populations grow. Humans are also a herd of tribal animals tending to stick with the common goals and beliefs of the herd even if they don't think about or even believe in them.[2] Wherever there is conflict, people will move elsewhere for their own self-protection.

Considerable data on migration movements are available, more easily now than before, because data are updated and provided online.[3] The essential feature in urban planning is whether the migration is planned or forced, given that both types have a socioeconomic connection. Planned migration brings with it some funding to support the migrants, whereas forced movement, as in situations involving conflict or natural calamity, usually leaves those people in need of financial and accommodation assistance. The migration swings have also linked to major wars and conflicts over the centuries bringing with them how this will translate into possible conflicts over coming centuries as travel becomes easier and contacts more fluid. The guiding issue for the future, based on both past and present experience, is whether through calamity or otherwise, there will be genuine refugees fleeing from persecution (Jews under Nazis and Christians currently from Islamic territories) or economically disadvantaged people fleeing as economic migrants. Again, much of this has always stemmed from politics, with for example, the start of the October 2018 "Caravan" of economic migrants marching up from mainly Honduras through Mexico to the United States.

The *Migration and Remittances Factbook* of 2011 puts annual migration at just over 35 percent of the global population, but this cannot be seen as an overall average as it also varies from time to time according to whether women and families are included. Estimates made by the United Nations High Commission for Refugees vary according to the percentage of migrants that are refugees, suggesting over 7 percent, but these figures are difficult to verify.

---

[2]Religions were created from early days and later used to control populations by introducing the concept of heaven and hell and the afterlife: do as I say—heaven; don't do as I say—hell.

[3]United Nations. n.d. "Global Migration Database." http://www.un.org/en/development/desa/population/migration/data/empirical2/index.shtml

The planning conundrum in relation to mass migration, as has been seen through past and present wars, is how this can suddenly put a strain on the provision of resources and infrastructure, when infrastructure typically needs to be planned for years ahead.

Regional

Regional migration is dominated by the availability and location of jobs, while influenced by immigration policies where certain countries prohibit immigration, and certainly citizenship. Again, this is governed by financial policies; for example, some countries wishing to restrict the wealth to their own citizens as in China, Japan,[4] and Korea in Asia, and Poland, Austria, or Switzerland, in Europe. Other countries such as Australia with a small population base, encourage immigration to widen the tax base.

Structurally, there is substantial migration from the northern, that is, the European Union, countries, from those with lower to those with higher incomes, whereas in America the long-term trend has been from the south to the north. Furthermore, while it is normal to see people moving from the developing to the developed countries, the United Nations Population Fund cites recent figures showing that as much as 43 percent of the migration is from one developing country to another.

The relevance of urban planning to regional population movement, or its lack thereof, lies in a country's ability to match its long-term infrastructure objectives to a known, or at least calculable growth rate. In the Australian case for example, estimated growth rates in the two major cities of Melbourne and Sydney were far exceeded many years ahead of schedule. By 2018, Sydney's population had attained a level that had been predicted to be reached only 30 years later. As a result, infrastructure, especially roads, has fallen far short of the required level while house prices have soared. At the same time, Australia has also been complaining about immigration levels exceeding the capacity of the major cities to handle the inflow and has been trying to come up with policies to force immigrants to live in rural areas. This policy, however, has not had much traction

---

[4]Japan Announced Relaxation of Immigration Laws due to Work Force Shortages, *CNN*, November 2, 2018.

since the immigration is largely family related in that the immigrants wish to live near their relatives; it is not possible to force people to live in the countryside if there are no employment opportunities.

As populations continue to expand, there will likely be an urban drift that will blur the boundaries between interlinking cities. In addition, in the foreseeable future people's choice of where people want to live appears likely to be driven by considerations of where they can maintain an income, whether from the government or from paid employment.

The hitherto unresolved issue in this regional migration centers on the sheer size of the potential movements, certainly away from conflict but mainly with people seeking a better life than is possible in their countries of origin. This has previously seen large attempted migrations to Europe, seriously impacting the living standards of the host country. Such migrations seek regions that are not merely "better" but "much better"; where for example, the recent "migrant caravan" from Honduras marching through Mexico to the United States were offered resettlement in Mexico, but this was rejected since they wanted American benefits. Similarly, Australian "boat people"[5] transferred to Nauru declined relocation to the United States, where they would have had to work wanting to remain on welfare should predicted future job losses continue, this wave of migrants seeking a better life might become overwhelming and fraught with political consequences.

Country-Specific Predictions

It is predicted that in the next 50 years Africa will have the highest rate of population growth, India's ranking second. This raises certain issues in the light of India already being overpopulated in relation to its infrastructure and Africa lagging behind in meeting its infrastructural needs anyway. An interesting but plausible rationale for the pace of development in Africa is that although populations are controlled by governments that are able to control essential resources such as water and food, governments in most populated African countries governments did not control the water

---

[5]People attempting to arrive by boat from Indonesia were relocated to Nauru in line with Australian government policy.

supply and, there was sufficient fertile ground for people to throw down seeds to and grow their own food. This therefore reduced government's ability to control the local population or tax them, thereby limiting the volume of revenue available for spending on infrastructure.

Through the 1960s and the remnants of the Cold War, both the United States and Russia contested for influence across Africa until the prevailing economic constraints tended to demonstrate that there was nothing to be gained politically in seeking support from leaders who often showed no loyalty. Since then, China has taken over and from one end of Africa to the other has simply gone in to deal directly with the people in power and funded infrastructure projects carried out by Chinese nationals. This went against other donors who were trying to be helpful but were constrained by a complicated, top-heavy, and outmoded bidding process.[6] This will have major implications for urban planning in the future on two fronts—first, in the provision of infrastructure that was unaffordable locally, and, second, the question of what China will expect in exchange for its largesse.[7] Not unnaturally, China will want something and as with everything else involving China, they are not constrained by political cycles and can wait.[8]

Species Evolvement

Darwin's theory of evolution points out that animal species will continue to evolve and that in the process of evolution they will either adapt or die out. Some have already gone extinct and are unlikely to ever be replaced unless they are cloned. The question then becomes, to what extent does the global population need to plan to protect the surviving species from extinction, and what needs to be done to provide space for those that are endangered?

---

[6] P.J. Nelson & Co. Pty Ltd., Strategy Consultants. Up to 30 percent can be spent on processing grants, and low-interest loans tend to favor the developer.

[7] In August 2018, the Chinese premier hosted a large group of African leaders in Beijing.

[8] Xi Jinping was elected president in 2013; he appears to have established a long-term hold on the position in a country that tends to hold on to leaders and the state machinery works behind them.

Recent estimates predict that half of the known vertebrates have become extinct since 1970, largely owing to habitat loss from land clearing, livestock grazing, overhunting, and fishing.[9] Humans have played a major role in the stark declines in wildlife populations around the planet over the past four-and-a-half decades, according to a report published by the World Wildlife Fund in October 2018.[10] The same cause could also apply to the disappearance of plants. The question that confronts humans is whether they want to continue to see these animals, since long gone are the days when African safaris made it possible to watch game in their natural habitat without a lion or cheetah surrounded by a dozen minivans. Will human evolution progress to a point where they eventually have to visit "A tree museum"?[11] On the one hand, animals are being contained so as not to disadvantage humans, while at the same time special enclosures and zoos are being constructed to attempt to recreate natural environments, though without the open spaces.

In regard to human evolution, major changes can be expected in the way they develop and in what will be required to accommodate them. Longevity will increase, but as can be seen in some demographics, certain populations are afflicted with weight issues that are apparent even at a glance.

Obesity measures based on Body Mass Index (BMI) indicate that obesity has nearly doubled since 1980 and that in 2008 more than 1.4 billion adults aged 20 and older were overweight. Of these, over 200 million men and nearly 300 million women were obese. Worldwide, overweight and obesity are said to be the fifth leading risk for deaths through diabetes and heart disease. Furthermore, around 40 million children under the age of five were overweight in 2011.[12] Meanwhile, data released by the Center for Disease Control (CDC) suggest obesity is more prevalent in lower socioeconomic groups, confirming concerns that this is related to dietary issues exacerbated by easy access to take-away or so-called "junk food,"

---

[9]Zoological Society of London, 2017.

[10]The report is based on the Living Planet Index, which takes stock of the Earth's biodiversity by examining 16,704 populations of more than 4,000 vertebrate species around the world.

[11]From Joni Mitchell's song, *Big Yellow Taxi*, 2002.

[12]European Association for Study of Obesity.

which forms a regular part of diet in those groups. In the Philippines, the number of overweight children under five years old has increased by as much as 400 percent since 2013.[13]

This increasing obesity trends would indicate that future populations will become sedentary and that urban planning has to provide for facilities such as gymnasiums, or build and plan such that people are forced to walk more, or, if such measures fail, they will need to set up facilities that simply cater to an evolving body size. The danger is that the younger generation has become immersed in technology to the extent that it has taken over their lives completely. This is quite apparent evidenced by typical behavior where young people congregate who barely talk to one another busy on their devices. This complacency can be harmful in that individuals conveniently avoid facing real-life challenges.

In future, part of the question of species evolvement will be tied to connectivity; where people will be linked to one another voluntarily and will be able to communicate without having to press buttons or hold phones, merely by using a device implanted in their body. This will also lead to their becoming "globally chipped" beings, citizens to whom governments can communicate instructions through a chip implanted in their bodies. Already, some governments have controllers in tunnels, for example, where they can override phone conversations or music to warn drivers of dangers ahead. Taking that to the next level, such interruptions will become routine, with governments being able to instruct, control, and govern their citizens through messages communicated to the devices implanted in citizens' bodies. These developments will allow governments to increase their control over the lives and movement patterns of citizens, not to mention the capacity to identify earnings, track taxation streams, and carry out policing in general.

What this points toward is greater social connectivity relating also to government control, which, although perhaps abhorrent to current populations, may seem perfectly normal to future generations, particularly since, as it would appear, most people are content with accessing their social media platforms and indifferent to what the hosts are doing with the information gathered. The suggestion, therefore, is that, but for

[13]Reported by CNN, April 2016.

sporadic complaints, people 100 years hence will by and large have come to accept government's electronic intrusion.

Human Culling

While not an attractive subject for discussion, human culling is nothing new, from the distant past, to Nazi Germany's ethnic cleansing of Jews and gypsies, up to the Chinese one-child policy, which has seen the aborting of millions of female fetuses, leaving the country with 40 million more males than females. Suffice it to say that this behavior can happen and could be applied from different perspectives, given an expanding or overwhelming population.

As China was faced with the situation of having more people than their development plans could accommodate, the one-child policy was brought in, curbing population growth. This was simply introduced by government as a law rather than by inducement, in contrast to the case in India, where men were offered transistor radios if they agreed to have a vasectomy. This is culling at the conception end. Of course, with the preoccupation with having sons, female fetuses were aborted.

In America, the abortion versus antiabortion debate continues, underguided by Christian principles in regard to the sanctity of life, which is not considered an issue by countries without a religious base. There is also the general call for birth control education, but little progress seems to have been made, as reflected by the spectacle of refugee camps being swamped with multitudes of women and children bereft of male support or any other means of support beyond official aid.

Next consider the removal of "undesirables," or antisocial elements such as criminals, and Philippine President Rodrigo Duterte's war on drug dealers and addicts springs to mind. What amounted to execution became acceptable in law, with no review. Similarly, in China, as well as in some other Asian and Arab states, what might be considered minor crimes in other countries can bring with them death sentences. In some instances, whole families were executed. This manipulation through controlling births actually goes beyond the crimes themselves; punitive measures are carried out to instill fear in the general population and keep them under control. All of this is a form of social engineering and raises the very important issue of whether governments will in future allow some sections of the population to simply breed and then go on social welfare or whether drastic measures will be enforced.

At the other end of forced control over conception is social engineering of old age. The 20th-century superrich are investing heavily in making extensions to their longevity, but this is as yet also superexpensive, and likely to be so for some time. Thus, while the wealthy may in future live to an older age, it is likely that the less well-off will not match this target or be physically or mentally able to remain productive members of the community.[14] Age might still limit a person's ability to work or generate income. It may be possible to live off income from investments but unlikely when a body is worn out.

All progressive countries have antidiscrimination laws that supposedly protect the aged, but none are actually followed; hence, anyone over 65 years old in the West finds it hard to get employment;[15] all of this has gotten worse since computerized monitoring of job applications automatically rejects people beyond a certain age. Governments also have trouble balancing their finances since old-age pensions were set against life expectancy targets that are exceeded. Hence, people are not dying when planned for, and pensions have to be paid for longer periods.

Culling the aged, while unpleasant to admit, is a fairly simple task for governments. Aside from the fact that human habitats have become too small to include aged family members to be looked after by their siblings, only relatively few retirees can afford retirement villages, and those that can often do not receive the care they expect.[16] Moreover, it is possible for governments to manipulate savings and pension plans for self-funded retirees, while those on welfare can have benefits reduced so that it is impossible for them to live. Another alternative is to simply raise the retirement age, expecting a brick layer to be still physically capable of

---

[14]Just by adjusting access and cost of medical insurance, one can decide who lives and who dies.

[15]This was confirmed by the author through an extensive study of the EU system.

[16]Australia announced the establishment of a Royal Commission into Aging in September 2018.

laying bricks into old age. This extended aging presents a major financial problem.

Consequently, more and more governments are introducing voluntary euthanasia[17] laws, making voluntary dying more common, while at the other extreme people want to live forever. While different countries have different laws and in some countries assisted dying is considered illegal, doctors have long helped suffering patients to end their lives, and it's possible to simply go to another country to carry out one's wish to die. The main limiting factor in "death migration" is really the stigma to be borne by the bereaved family members and some of the legal ramifications concerning property surrounding an act deemed to be unlawful.[18]

These enforced or facilitated culling techniques can be employed under the radar by making it difficult or untenable to continue to live, but a totalitarian government could simply decree termination of those over a certain age. The 2120 question comes up again: Will people by then be OK with voluntary death and just accept culling as a way of life, or death?

---

[17]The term is avoided in Germany given its Second World War connotations.
[18]The U.S. law apparently excludes death duties for people at sea, fostering the old-age cruise industry.

CHAPTER 4

Urban Planning

Overall Aim

Looking for a guide to overall planning, the millennium development goals (MDGs) were the eight international development goals for the year 2015 that had been established after the millennium summit of the United Nations in 2000, following the adoption of the United Nations Millennium Declaration. All 191 United Nations member states at that time, and at least 22 international organizations, committed themselves to helping achieve the following development goals by the year 2015:

1. To eradicate extreme poverty and hunger.
2. To achieve universal primary education.
3. To promote gender equality and empower women.
4. To reduce child mortality.
5. To improve maternal health.
6. To combat HIV/AIDS, malaria, and other diseases.
7. To ensure environmental sustainability.
8. To develop a global partnership for development.

Unfortunately, making goals does not in itself achieve the objective, and they lose their effectiveness when stated without any indication of the possibility of their being achieved. Eradication of extreme poverty and hunger would have been a known impossible target, whereas generalities calling for improvement would have been a different matter. Urban development in this narrative is mainly the ensuring of environmental sustainability within the overall context.

Internationally, the important achievements for addressing climate change–related hazards as part of urban development targets include the

UN Framework Convention on Climate Change (UN-FCCC 1992), the Kyoto Protocol (1997), the Hyogo Framework for Action (2005), and the Paris Agreement (2015). Urban planning is developed within the foregoing context, but, again, while outlining erstwhile goals, will the population on the planet continue pursuing similar vague goals, will government on an international scale have become more definitive, and will some process evolve to ensure implementation?

Definition

Global strategic planning (GSP), as attested to by Wikipedia, is a process adopted by international organizations to formulate an effective global strategy. It is a process of evaluating the internal and external environments by multinational organizations and making decisions about how they will achieve their objectives. GSP differs from domestic strategic planning in that in the former process organizations consider internal as well as external environments. In fact, the external environment is a more crucial consideration at the global than at the domestic level because crime and pollution on one side of a wall soon spill over on to the other.

Urban planning is a technical and political process concerned with the development and design of (diminishing) land use in an urban environment covering issues of air, water, and accompanying infrastructure coming in and out of the area. With **public welfare** as its primary concern, it deals with the physical layout of human settlements as well as sanitation, protection, and use of the environment. The big question in this objective both now and for the future is, just what is this broad concept of **public welfare**?

The public welfare concept has undergone a considerable change since its earlier conception as merely an end measure,[1] while the dictionary defines it as good fortune, health, happiness and prosperity, etc.[2] This presents a wide aspiration to plan toward.

---

[1]Hansen, John E., Social Welfare History Project (1935 to 1996). The term used to denote the different tax-supported programs that provide cash assistance or services to individuals and families who are deemed eligible on the basis of their income and assets (USA) 2014.

[2]www.dictonary.com

Rationale

As has been demonstrated historically, dangers creep in when human habitants do not live in controlled spaces. For early human tribes living in sparsely populated areas, it was acceptable to live in one spot and, when this became polluted, to move on.

Once people settled in specific areas, issues with sanitation and rubbish collection, including collection of corpses, developed. Serious issues resulted, such as plagues, the first recorded of one being an Egyptian outbreak followed by the *first pandemic* originating in Africa, hitting Europe in 541 AD; the *second pandemic,* "Black Death," originated in China in 1334 and spread along the trade routes through Constantinople to Europe, wiping out an estimated 33 percent of the European population. Bubonic plagues actually continued sporadically through Europe for some time afterward and were confined mainly to Italy.

Once the cause of the pandemics was recognized (rather than being seen as divine retribution), steps had to be taken to improve sanitation and remove pests such as rats. Urban planning began around the local ruler's castle or fortress, where people could live and tend their crops and livestock but where locals could retreat to the castle for safety in times of danger. In ancient times, the local rulers owned the land, which they allowed people to live on and use for a consideration. Since the ruler owned the land, and therefore the housing, he could exert pressure on the tenants to maintain their dwellings, and even till recently in parts of Europe outdoor plumbing still existed. Overall, a large part of initial planning came from fortification requirements.

As the rulers owned the land, they were able to set some of it aside for their own leisure (and hunting), which their tenants were eventually able to take advantage of. Similar situations currently exist with government parks open to the public. In centrally planned economies, such as China and Vietnam, ownership is vested in the government, which replaces the landowners of the past.

Countries have progressed further with urban planning, and governments have their subjects registered in one way or the other in order to control (or plan) settlements for the future. In some countries such as China and, recently, Vietnam, all residents were restricted to their own areas, usually from birth, and were subject to police checks if they attempted to move out. While this restriction has largely been eased, with the need for people to find work, until 2017 the Chinese one-child policy existed, and any subsequent child was *unregistered* and hence received no benefits. China is now moving toward a system of having its population identified on facial recognition systems so as to be able to determine where anyone is at any time. Obviously, the ability to have the entire population registered in a database will help contribute to urban planning requirements and aid law enforcement, but it can only be hoped that the laws thereby enforced are benevolent.

It should be noted that each generation comes in with a different reference point. In Australia, for example, the government attempted to bring in a national identity card in 1985, but this was voted down in a referendum held in 1987, as atrocities committed during the Second World War were still in living memory. Various other kinds of ID systems were then sneaked in so that, one way or the other, everyone is now documented under some government system, driving license, tax file number, and, recently, a database access to all medical records. This is something current teenagers do not object to, with some even thinking that the government's collection of this information or having access to it for its own purposes is not exceptional.[3] In other words, they know and expect to be manipulated and are ready to accept being told that this is in their best interests. Progress this forward 100 years, and what else will that generation believe is normal, acceptable, and in their own best interests?

Components—The Urban Basics

The following are the basic living (or existing) requirements that need to be incorporated into an expanding urban development base in line with basic objectives of public welfare.

---

[3]A survey shows that 41 percent of Americans do not know what Auschwitz was, April 12, 2018, www.ABC7news.com

Air

This is a prime requisite, without which no humans can breathe. Not long ago, it had been unthinkable that in developed countries people would have to be carrying bottled water and that in some countries tap water was dangerous to drink. Similarly, air is considered a free natural resource, but it is likely that even this will become restricted, and in certain regions, especially Asia, people are already going about their daily travel wearing masks and, in some cases, having these with their own air supply.

Governments are now responding to this threat to some degree, although it is still questionable whether sufficient attention is being given to the matter. When people fall sick or, as in certain capitals, when it rains and sulphur or dust spots stain cars, public awareness is stirred and pressure exerted on governments. On the other hand, in countries such as Bangladesh, particularly in Dhaka, where air pollution can be seen to be well above acceptable limits, government financial priorities can be elsewhere and the problem is unaddressed.

Water

Again, one hundred years ago no one would have thought that in 2018 some people would have to rely on bottled water or imagined how a city itself could run out of water.[4] This has happened and could be a sign for the future. Already, many cities in the world lack piped drinking water, and even in cities where water is considered drinkable people prefer bottled water, which is more expensive than fuel for their cars.

The issue of water has many dimensions. The first is simply to provide enough drinking water, and the second relates to what needs to be done if insufficient water is predicted. Currently, there are ways of desalinating (removing salt from) seawater to make it fit for humans and animals to drink, but this, again, not only comes at a monetary cost but also increases the salinity of seawater, which in turn affects marine life.

---

[4]Cape Town predicted it would run out of water in mid-2018 but has now put this off to "sometime in 2019," meanwhile almost doubling water prices and publicly shaming water wasters. www.capetown.gov.za/thinkwater

The first remedial step should obviously be in the direction of conservation and then recycling.

A less palatable form of drinking water is recycled sewage, whose use, in the first instance, has been promoted for industries and gardens but not advertised where it is already fed into normal urban water supply systems to some degree or another.

A less obvious issue in regard to water availability but linked to wastewater is the effect already being felt on groundwater and its contamination in low-lying areas, where untreated effluent has already contaminated the water table, making the water undrinkable, and this has extended to other areas affected by "fracking."[5]

While it is undeniable that water is essential for humans, it should also be seen as necessary for animals and for industrial use and, obviously, for supporting crops and producing food in general. Major issues are emerging in this area along with industry and food supply being usurped by the need for residential land.

Wastewater

While the importance of water is unquestionable, removal of wastewater (or shit) is also necessary, given the potential for pestilence and disease. This is linked to the perceived future of water availability and the need to consider converting wastewater into "usable water."

Not to be forgotten is the aforementioned problem that untreated wastewater can filter into groundwater, contaminating the only source of usable water for many, especially poor, families. This too is a planning issue, affecting as it does people in low-lying or delta areas, where there is no flowoff, such areas already being at sea level.

Food

In regard to urban development, rural–urban migration will have a direct impact on food production. This has various components, from reducing

---

[5]Injecting liquid at high pressure underground in order to open fissures, releasing oil or gas.

the land available for agriculture to individuals finding it less attractive to live in rural areas vis-a-vis urban centers. It also increases the likelihood that more chemicals will be used to stimulate production, with possible negative side effects.

Similar considerations involve fisheries, both sea and fish farms. Fishing stocks have already become seriously depleted in some areas, with some practices likely to wipe out vast resources.[6] The fish and shrimp farming industry, which had an impressive beginning, especially in the poorer countries, is now suffering from diseases that have crept in and from chemicals introduced to attempt to control them.[7] On the positive side, the Norwegians have started salmon farms, and the Japanese have overcome tuna farm problems, specifically, fish in ponds killing one other accidentally, by now having them swim in continuous circular motion.

There is an issue regarding not only food source, but also the way in which food will be prepared, consumed, and delivered, leading to trends in eating out and even in restaurant construction. Already, a number of innovative methods have emerged, such as more and more people eating out or at least sourcing their food from outside. On the one hand, the McDonald's business model is being extended to various replicas that are now called restaurants instead of "take-aways," and these have progressed to the point where customers are allowed to preorder, drive through, or have deliveries through "Uber eats." Trials have been run on delivery of orders by drones, but these, while likely to be commonplace in future, still require resolution of some technical and legal issues. The issue of concern should be the close proximity of these fast food providers, reducing the need for people's mobility in order to get fed.

Shelter

People have to live somewhere, so the type of housing in their habitat will be important. Along with this will be not just the style or density of housing but also its ownership. For example, if the hypothesis is true that

---

[6]Japan Tuna is still long-lining off the Southern Australian coast for Tuna during mating.

[7]Both China and Vietnam have suffered in this area.

there will be AI-induced job losses in future, driving people onto social welfare, will it be necessary for government to provide housing as part of welfare, or will a set payment to all unemployed be sufficient for them to acquire their own housing? Current home ownership figures are misleading since in a majority of cases not the resident but the financier or bank is the actual owner holding the title until the mortgage is discharged.[8] So instead of ownership, if the poor rent their own housing, what sort of housing would be inexpensive enough to be affordable?

Once humans have their viable habitats, they will want to move between theirs and others'. This brings with it the communication corridors provided by walkways, roads and highways, rail links, airports, and water transport. Each of these means of interconnection brings with it a multitude of issues as to how they could be best achieved, but the main consideration is that, first, people would rather not want to endure too long commutes to and from a job and so will want less congested roads, high-speed rail, and conveniently located airports. Those with cars will either want to have somewhere to park or to be able to do away with them altogether. Otherwise, they will want to live in a way that somehow negates the need for "unnecessary" travel. Perhaps people will move along tubes between buildings to do away with the need to walk?[9] Again, a big question will be whether in the event that easy access is not possible, populations would consider it natural and acceptable to travel for many hours a day to and from work just to have a job.

For roads and rail there can be various offsets in relation to costs. Toll roads can be quicker, but one has to pay, as for high-speed trains, tubular trains, and special highways. Then there are the new aspects for future dwellings, where everything is at walking distance. Or one can take the case of new ships built on which people make their permanent home as they drift around the world and need to walk only around the decks or on treadmills in the floating gym.

---

[8]It is a good marketing ploy for governments to be able to talk about how well their economies are doing with high private home ownership, when in fact the real ownership remains with the banks.

[9]Some department stores have these between floors as a novelty, but the system could be extended.

People can now adjust their living environment by means of the connectivity available through the Internet and various social media. It is possible to have a meeting with people in Europe, Africa, and Australia all from one office; someone driving off to drop kids at baseball can use a mobile, then a speaker phone while driving back home, and then get back on the computer; while another person has left the office and is on the way home, all without a break in conversation.

It is also possible to avoid having to bother to type into a computer or to read the text yourself; and something can be translated from or into a wide selection of languages. Astonishingly, in September 2018, a team in the United States demonstrated brain linkages between three people playing checkers, making moves by mind linkage alone. What all this means is that the days of clocking in nine to five on a job will soon be a thing of the past, and future inhabitants of the Earth will have their personal lifestyles integrated against an office-related dimension.

From present indications, it is clear that the connectivity just discussed is assuming increasing importance in individuals' lives and is not only here to stay but likely to increase. Technological advancement is certain to replace mobile devices with some form of holographic system that makes it possible for people to dispense with carrying machines around with them and use implants instead.[10]

While all this connectivity has many advantages unheard of during the "snail mail" era of 100 years ago and while algorithms can predict people's preferences based on data collected from voting and shopping patterns, it can also bring with it dangers that might not yet have emerged. As an illustration of this, Google announced a joint exercise with China on October 15, 2018, at an event hosted by *WIRED* unveiling its *Project Dragonfly*, where it will roll out a Chinese version of Google that will grant China access to all of its citizens' data and presumably all of Google's other material. This effectively means that the Chinese government will have details on the majority of the people on the planet who are using or have used Google. And how many people have not used Google? Such a government could easily control where and how people live.

---

[10]One man in Sydney, in 2018, had his rail pass embedded in his skin so that he could go through turnstiles.

Under international law, ownership of land as construed by those in power at the time, as many indigenous societies can attest, depends on claiming territory and then having the ability and means to enforce the claim. As discussed in the context of mortgages, while people generally feel that their ownership gives them title to land that they have bought, in reality this is only subtenure under a sovereign government, where in exchange the tenant can be taxed in one form or another, as were the serfs of old. The question is whether this so-called "ownership" system will continue into the future or whether there will be a need for an increased supply of subsidized social housing, putting the balance of visible ownership back on governments? If the latter, this will determine what standard habitats might become under a cost–benefit model. A likely outcome would be the multitude of identical high-rise complexes covering Hong Kong.

Otherwise, for an individual's living requirements, if dependent on the size of habitat, although this is likely to become smaller, it is certain that it will be adequately wired to interface with the resident to take over many of the physical functions currently performed. Just as the TV remote removes the need to press buttons, so will most habitat appliances respond to voice controls, perhaps even giving reminders and offering suggestions. The danger here, as with many futuristic possibilities, is that people may become immersed in the technology and move away from reality. In other words, they could turn out to be more comfortable conversing with machines than with people.[11]

Education

In future it is likely that teaching methods in schools will follow a different format as well as not relying on an established syllabus. Part of this requirement, according to the latest predictions, is that the next generation will likely have 17 different subject-level employments[12] and 40 employers in a lifetime.

---

[11]Many studies already show people spend more time on computers, devices, and phones than conversing with others.

[12]Instead of being just an accountant, they might also work in a restaurant, do some coding, and drive an Uber.

Consequently, as with the new experimental Lindfield Learning Village in Sydney, Australia, teaching will happen around "waterholes" or campfires. Students will take responsibility for their own learning. Then "high schoolers" will mentor the kindy kids. Lindfield will take a "stage" not "age" approach, in which students advance on the basis of their progress rather than their year level. Pupils will be divided into K-12 "home bases" of about 350 to encourage a sense of belonging in what could otherwise be an overwhelming campus. Older students will be encouraged to not just mentor but teach younger ones. Each student will have his or her own "learning pathway," monitored by a "learning mentor," and the school will teach through projects that engage several disciplines together rather than focusing on one at a time. For example, a robot project might engage math, computer technology, science, and, if they create an imaginary story for their robot, English.[13] Similar teaching concepts have been introduced in other countries, especially Scandinavia, where Finland as a leader is said to have one of the best learning rates.

The development demand will involve a cost in turning around institutional classroom design to one based on the more progressive model.[14] This is likely to take some time since government planners have always liked to put issues into boxes that cover everyone. This was usually because they had to gather statistics, which were not always easy to compile, while now data is readily available and can be adjusted to develop more than a single model.

Part of the hypothesis behind new learning methods is that there is less need to learn *facts* since almost any of these can be simply searched online. Does anyone really need to remember who the 13th president of the United States was?[15] Learning itself, according to leading educators, should be directed toward exploring what to do with the facts, not memorizing them.

This open form of teaching and interpretation of facts rather than retention has always been a concept in universities or higher education

---

[13]School Opening in 2019, *Sydney Morning Herald*, July 13, 2018.
[14]The Lindfield experimental school received ten times the number of applications for available spaces.
[15]Millard Fillmore 1950–1953.

and will continue in the same vein as followed by schools. The emphasis here will be on expansion of disciplines and the qualifications attached to them in order to meet future changes in lifestyles. Job requirements will need to become part of the driving force that determines the syllabuses if there are to be fewer employment prospects.

Education, overall, will acquire an IT focus, bringing with it an entirely new vocabulary and abbreviations.

Recreation

Among the ancillary requirements for essential human habitats, though receiving less attention, is urban access to recreational facilities. On the one hand, there have to be massive stadiums for competitive games to provide an outlet for large numbers of people, as the Romans found long ago, since governments have always needed to provide distractions for their subjects. These stadiums need to be conveniently accessible from public habitation via road and rail, with parking facilities, and they face all the health, plumbing, and security issues of a modern world. Attending these events incurs costs, and if spectators are not the ones getting exercise on the playing field, as are their gladiators, they do get exercise getting to and from the event.

Day-to-day living is increasingly focused around malls or shopping centers as well as, in some countries, 7-Elevens, which, while attracting people to shop, nevertheless provide recreational areas, with some malls or shopping centers now featuring indoor skydiving facilities or, as in Hanoi, underground swimming and ice-skating complexes.

These large facilities come at a cost and, consequently, should have provision for people to have access to free-range areas such as parks and beaches to just sit and relax.[16] Again, with increased populations, accessibility and parking at such venues can become costly. More and more recreational spaces are being lost, especially near urban centers, with bowling greens and community centers being demolished to make way for high-rise developments. Certain golf clubs face a similar fate, but

---

[16]Shopping centers or malls try to make it easy to get in but difficult to get out of shops, while limiting seating so people have to either use restaurants or keep shopping.

wealthy members who can influence local council decisions provide a counterweight.

Dying

While not an attractive topic, again in the context of expanding populations, the number of people dying will also add further constraints on the availability of land. When there was ample land available for burial in line with religious customs, this did not create a major problem, but as habitats grew, cemeteries found themselves in the middle of high-rise developments.[17]

On the one hand, it is reassuring that living relatives can commemorate their deceased and tend their graves, but over time and through population movements people lose touch with their forebears, and graves are left unattended. Against this is the pressure from people who resent living around cemeteries as they are reminded of their future demise, while governments and developers view the land as unproductive, though having commercial potential.

The issue of disposal of human remains depends largely on attitude and, as with so much else, on its cost. Graves need to be tended and in many cases incur "rental" costs, whereas cremation is a one-off activity and expense, after which the living can grieve in their own time. The whole issue is linked to humans' concepts of the sanctity of life, but, as with many other perceptions, these can change over time and in relation to burial land availability, and people are resorting to adaptive ways of grieving even to the extent of rocketing ashes into space or mixing them with soil through which to plant trees. Previously options have been reviewed available to the superrich, but it is noteworthy that some are paying to preserve their corpses in the hope that some future technology might bring them back to life. These remain in the minority.

Overall, the disposal of remains with its legal connotations remains an issue for urban planning, which, no matter how distasteful, still needs to be built into development models.

---

[17]Proximity to cemeteries seriously lowers land and apartment prices, especially among Asians.

Planning by Financial Status

All planning is related to affordability and priorities. It also has a major political dimension in that governments need to curry favor with their electors. Whereas major development projects involve investment over a number of years of implementation, these can then, in a democracy, extend beyond the lives of one government term. The problem with this is that governments want to win an election by promising things in the present, whereas the more logical process would be to stage expenditure over a longer period. Expediency suggests that politicians are not going to defer spending if they might no longer be in power.

Similarly, the answer to the question of where the planning money is to go will usually, in democratic countries, be where the greater voter demographic resides, so congestion in cities will always attract more attention than the plight of a few farmers spread over thousands of acres.[18] In a centrally planned country such as China, there are fewer restrictions. Either way, the wealthier people will always be able to find more attractive accommodation, and governments will move to adjust to their needs by being able to influence laws and regulations in their own interests. Examples would be where building restrictions can be imposed on high rises crowding an area or residency rules setting limits on how many students can live in a one-bedroom apartment.[19]

Within the city population it is politically expedient for politicians to back policies favoring homeless people being taken off the street, because while the homeless may not have many votes, those who do might find it offensive stepping over people sleeping on the pavements while on their way to work. Basically, all this is about urban development being tied to politics and the ownership and distribution of money. While this concept is unlikely to change in future, the question becomes whether the disparity between the rich and the rest will become more pronounced and how a diverse population will react to it.

---

[18]The small size of Singapore has constituencies on a few city blocks, enabling closer contact with voters.

[19]Sydney Strata Titles have had to allow rules to prevent multitudes of students being allowed to reside in a single apartment near universities.

CHAPTER 5

Move to Urban Environments

Forward Projections

The move toward urban environments is increasing and will continue. This drive is mainly because in the one instance it takes fewer farm laborers to produce food and milk, which earlier required substantial physical proximity, while, on the other, not only are jobs becoming scarcer per head of population but projections are that the one job for life is now outdated and in future people are likely to have perhaps 40 different roles through which to earn income, if they even have jobs at all.

The many different jobs that people are likely to have, if any, in future could be online, so it would not matter where they live, but people are more likely to be urban based, moving from one activity to the other. This means people will be forced to live in close proximity and with a limited availability of land, or of transport between settlements. This will set one of the parameters for future planning. Proximity also considers the multiplier effect, which roughly estimates that for every four workers one support person is required.

It is superfluous to lay out the statistics on the move to urban centers in order to support the increase in proximity since it has become obvious.

Clusters and Satellites

In describing a move to cities or urban environments, what takes place, in the first instance, is people moving to a central city, where they then drift into satellite areas when living there becomes too complicated or expensive. In big cities, police tend to move homeless people on and competition for jobs becomes increasingly fierce even if jobs are available.

The projection that people might, on the one hand, have up to 40 jobs in a lifetime, together with the likely need to move between these at the same time, suggests the possible need for physical connectivity between urban focal points. Otherwise, there emerge single-purpose enclaves such as Silicon Valley, in the United States, copied elsewhere. Clusters spring up around special purpose activities, as with the recent announcement of a new city adjacent to the proposed airport of Badger's Creek outside Sydney, Australia, designed to bring with it new jobs.

Mega Dominated Clusters

As with the Silicon Valley example, with IT playing such a dominant role at present and with super companies such as Amazon and Google capitalized at over $1 trillion, the future will probably see such companies with spin-offs providing employment while at the same time requiring an urban environment to facilitate them. To titillate future possibilities, Elton Musk announced that he is now digging a tunnel from his garage to his office as a way to get to work without facing traffic.

These mega clusters need not be constrained on a geographical basis but can, as in the case of Amazon, have global linkages interacting in a similar way in many countries.

In the past, certain industries tended to concentrate in specific parts of the largest cities, such as in the UK and its central financial hub or a similar district of Wall Street in the United States. Large newspapers used to congregate in specific areas, such as in Fleet Street in the UK, but this has largely dissipated through innovations in communications and cost factors.[1] Otherwise, the so-called "top end of town" still retains some attraction but is often no longer necessary for carrying out basic business functions even if addresses might still remain important.

Subnational City Clusters

In the past, governments have used subnational city clusters to support local industry. In cases where around suburbs such as Elizabeth, in South

---

[1]Global innovation is illustrated in the fact that a major Sydney daily newspaper is written in Australia, typeset in Bangladesh, and then printed for distribution back in Australia.

Australia, a housing development had been instigated to take pressure off Adelaide, without considering how the people would be employed, a major development in a car manufacturing industry was introduced to solve that problem. Obviously, creating such an industry out of nothing driven by government incentives leads to the offshoot of companies producing car components, and for a time this proved to be a solution. In the long run, however, it was discovered that imports, despite heavy tariffs, were still cheaper, and, consequently, vehicle production died in Australia. To solve that South Australian crisis, it was decided to switch from making cars to building submarines, and the first of these was awarded to a Swedish company with the provision of commercial offsets if they used workers and components supplied from Australia. The next bright idea was to buy the next submarines from the French and build them in Australia, but since these were nuclear powered, and Australian politicians shy away from anything nuclear, they will create jobs with offsets on the submarines as well and will then need to be converted back to diesel power.[2] In Western Australia, the mining industry, which has established its own cluster, has suffered major employment swings, suggesting that in the future workforce mobility will come into place. Workers had bought houses that became worthless when the jobs disappeared, so it is unlikely this will be repeated.

Overall, clusters will continue to be important and some will continue to exist. This was the case with the motor industry in Detroit, while history also shows that these can outlive their life spans, just as nightclubs become all the rage before patrons move on. Perhaps in 100 years the clusters will have reached Mars?

Fortified Clusters

In many countries, certain communities have introduced protected villages, that is, living surrounded by protective walls, surveillance, and armed guards. These concepts, driven by necessity, need to be built into future urban models. Building these communities around existing

---

[2] Even the Australian government has stated that the cost of retrofitting of existing nuclear plants will be enormous, but it suited the government's political agenda driven by the fear of public reaction against anything involving nuclear power.

residences is more difficult than initiating them under new developments where the latter are now automatically designed with their own security systems. An example of these is in Johannesburg, South Africa, where houses are barricaded behind razor wire and armed guards patrol. Similarly, in Tanzania and Kenya, the company Ultimate Security guarantees the dispatch of a team of guards to any house within 6 minutes after the panic buttons spread around your house are pressed, the point being that the death penalty applies to both armed robbery and murder, so thieves prefer not to leave witnesses.

In Manila, it is possible to drive around Forbes Park, a fortified village with ample housing hosting a polo club, onto the jam-packed main road EDSA, through to Roxas Boulevard, through the suburb of Ermita and within 15 minutes be in the slums of Tondo, where people live in cardboard huts. This description of the disparity in living conditions in the Philippines has to be qualified by the fact that while theft might be predominant in wealthy areas, among the poor habitats scavenging for unwonted material is commonplace, but the same people do not steal from each other.[3]

Whether the need for personal protection leads to an equitable environment for populations as a whole, not having to build for protection in slums, such segregation is fairly inevitable as future populations are exposed to income disparities. The wealthy will continue to be able to protect themselves, but the limiting factor here is that they will still need to move out of their enclaves, and not everyone can, like Elon Musk, dig a tunnel from his car garage to his office.[4]

For society, in general, the question becomes whether such slums will be permitted to continue if they pose a security threat to the wealthy or whether they will be torn down. In the latter case, a further question in regard to what can be done about resettling the slum dwellers.

White and Black Flight

While racial connotations make this difficult to discuss, certain particularly noticeable areas in America and Australia have become subject to

---

[3] The argument presented was that the poor people have little worth stealing.
[4] Announced that building of the tunnel began in September 2018.

what can be called "white flight," where upwardly mobile African Americans in the United States have moved in in increasing numbers, resulting in the base population moving out. On the reverse side, upwardly mobile African Americans who can now afford the trappings of a reasonable house are also fleeing some of the inner-city ghetto areas.

In dealing with flight generally, in the western suburbs of Sydney, Australia, now heavily populated by immigrants who don't speak English and form their own enclaves, Australians, the traditional English speakers, are moving out. The same is obvious also in the UK.

However, in regard to true "flight," a more poignant situation has been witnessed in South Africa, where white farmers are having their land confiscated, a situation akin to that which occurred in Zimbabwe, where they were physically driven away from it, and in some case murdered, all under sanction of the government. On purely racial grounds, the "whites" are having to flee to other countries, while those who have taken over their land are unable to make it productive, with the result that shortages of food and other essentials have arisen. Cape Town, for example, almost ran out of water in 2018 since urban planning has not kept up with the management shift.

While this racial social engineering can be explained as a reaction in South Africa against the former system of apartheid, where a minority can be seen to have treated the majority as inferiors, two *wrongs* have never made a *right, and* neither of these helps a country when not run by the most skilled managers. A split system leads to division and lack of harmony, bringing with it suspicion and planning designed to permeate and perpetuate the split. The question raised here in light of future planning becomes whether such situations will continue to increase or whether over time a more rational acceptance of integration could become the norm. It is to be hoped that future development chooses the best person for the job rather than someone on ethnic grounds.

In an attempt to predict future requirements, while racial integration has to become inevitable in some ways, with people living in close proximity, a large number of mobile individuals carry their issues with them when they move, perpetuating the same problems. The real problem is that people tend to attribute some of these issues that thwart integration to either race or religion, when in actuality it comes down to people having different lifestyles and interests. The reality is that a white middle-aged Anglo-Saxon banker living in London would have no common level of interest, except perhaps in sport, with a laborer from Afghanistan who spoke no English. This becomes not a question of racism but only a lack of common interest. Part of the answer to the need for coexistence lies in education, including teaching people that differences of opinion are perfectly acceptable and individuals can still get along with each other without having to think identically, provided each leaves the other alone and respects the laws of the country.

Urban Corridors

As with business clusters, urban corridors are those areas surrounding border checkpoints that bring with them their own import and export businesses.

Examples of urban corridors would include all entry and exit points, that is, ports and harbors and also approaches to airports. These corridors spawn considerable tourist linkages and require design considerations specifically targeted to circumstances. An example of this is the inundation of the major tourist attraction of Bali by tourists. Experts proffered the idea of building an all-encompassing hotel resort that would give tourists a taste of the island, with bus tours to local villages so that visitors could experience the country, to contain tourists' physical presence within the hotel complex.

In Europe before EU integration, there used to be business activity at border posts, all of which has died out. In Africa, border enclaves still exist with towns that sprang up when crossings were major events.

Clearing Slum Areas under UN Millennium Goals

Going back to the first UN Millennium Goal, *To eradicate extreme poverty and hunger,* this is directly linked to urban planning mandates requiring provision of facilities replacing slum areas. The problem with this urban planning goal of *clearing the slum areas* is that they exist because of the extreme poverty; that is, it is necessary to overcome the cause to achieve the outcome. And as they are in poverty mostly because they have no money, they have to be given facilities, including access to accommodation, to overcome this.[5] The difficulty is not even with clearing the slums or building new accommodation despite the cost but finding the land for the reclamation. The slums are usually spread over land unsuitable for major development, so it becomes a question of not just pulling down and rebuilding, but finding a new location, and this, because of unavailability and expense, is usually on city outskirts with which slum dwellers have no affinity.

People in slums have generally grown into them and acclimatized themselves to that medium. Surrounding them are their friends and how they manage survival. They generally do not want to move, and if force is used (governments hesitate to use this option since these people become generational welfare recipients), drift back to their old areas or live on the street.

Move Away from Urban Centers

In reaction to the pressures on urban existence, being displaced by some groups, or their needing to live in protected fortified villages, many people are trying to move against the urban migration pattern. The main problem with this, of course, is that to be able to move out of the cities, one either has to have independent resources, a source of income not dependent on physical presence, or be able to retire with sufficient resources to move and reestablish.

Rural villages are becoming more attractive for both older couples and new families, and this is being made possible through the Internet and the ability to work from home. This typical English village concept is being copied in other areas such as Bundaroon, 2 hours' drive out of Sydney, which has all the necessary trappings of English village life. The problem here is that while the locals are enjoying their lifestyle, despite their best efforts to avoid publicizing its idyllic features, more and more people are attracted by the idea of getting away from the city, which, ultimately, will have to overwhelm the initial concept of that community as overall population numbers increase.

---

[5]P. Nelson. 2018. *UBI and the Threat to Democracy as We know it* (New York, NY: Business Expert Press).

While some people would enjoy the move from the city, recent studies (2018) show that Australia's attempts to plan against excessive immigration and for new arrivals to be moved out of the cities to the rural regions have met with little success since migrants coming from primitive living conditions consider these to be normal and prefer living in proximity to others of their ethnic origin rather than out in the open spaces.

Implication of Population Migrations

In recent times, large populations of people have moved from one continent to another as well as within continents as both refugees and economic migrants. This brings with it a short-term effect as well as longer-term consequences that need to be considered in the planning process. The effect is hard to predict. These movements bring with them major planning issues since while as in Australia the catchphrase was assimilation, early on postwar migrants had to mix with the locals and learn the language whereas more recently after large enclaves of foreigners were brought to the country and all lived together in the same areas, they no longer had a need to learn the local language, could shop and work in their own suburbs and consequently this assimilation failed.[6]

The separation and establishment of clusters has also received impetus from religious backgrounds, with Muslim immigrants fleeing the turmoil in their own countries bringing their religion and customs with them. These immigrants will also want their own places of worship, and this can challenge the dominant religion.

Looming large over the view 100 years from now, therefore, is the question of whether this religious separation will have taken further hold or whether a more enlightened generation will espouse the view that religions were meant to be allegorical and so people can see them for what they are and do not need to live strictly within the boundaries of their faith.

---

[6]The Australian 2018 census reported that now around 10 percent of Australians claim Asian origin. Over one million of 25 million are said to speak no English.

Job Loss Implications

Since it has already been postulated that all urban planning considerations are linked with the ability to fund them, the most critical issue pertains to the global population's ability to afford to live anywhere. While in the past it might have been possible to find a plot of land somewhere to build a hut and then continue to live off the land, this is now impossible for everyone. Everywhere there are governments that tax everything, and it's not possible to decide not to pay for electricity, barbecue in the backyard instead of using gas, and get rainwater for survival. Depending on where one lives, all of these activities can be governed by laws against being able to avoid paying to live and driving people to where they have to be taxed. Avoiding specific taxes doesn't work either since even if it were possible to avoid all other taxes, a value added or general service tax would be inevitable since almost anything that is bought attracts such a tax.

The overall implication in regard to this necessity for money is that people will need an income. It also means that some people will have more, others less, but planning will need to consider providing for the bottom tier. This in turn raises the question of how many of them there will be to support and how these lower income earners or welfare recipients can be integrated within the general community without creating logical frictions between them and whether in the end the process introduces laws reducing everyone in the population to the lowest common denominator. This is already a feature of daily living, leading to what is seen as the "nanny state," where knee jerk political reaction restricts personal freedoms.[7]

This raises the fact that some of the greatest minds of the century have predicted that at least 80 percent of the world's workforce will be replaced by computers or artificial intelligence, the only uncertainty being how long it will be before this happens. The average prediction on timing of losses appears to be about 30 years, but many believe it will be sooner. Regardless of the exact time frame, the impact on the planet will eventually be enormous because governments will still need to find a

---

[7]This is demonstrated by legislation introduced to protect people for their own stupidity, such as having a toe caught in a bath plughole, leading to a law governing the size of plug holes.

way to provide the unemployed with money on which to live.[8] This will again have an enormous effect on the quality of housing available and how people will be forced to live.

Health

One of the basic goals in life hinges not just on individual but on collective health. Health, however, has many dimensions, including the undefinable "happiness" quotient. There remain many components of this to be considered. Is being alive sufficient?

Physical

Following on from what might be the changes wrought by either job losses or people becoming less physically active is the impact on both physical and mental health. In the last hundred years, for example, although some incredible feats of physical endurance have been accomplished, the population in general has not been as physically active as it once was. Obviously, many contributing factors have led to this overall picture, but lack of exercise surely looms large among them, given that most people walk less. This has been aggravated by dangers in the street preventing children moving unescorted or from walking to and from school, and as cities become more crowded and crime can't be eradicated completely, this problem is bound to increase further.

A major contributing factor is the impact of the multibillion-dollar useless weight loss industry, which is not going to give in easily, while there is no government database that can reference which, if any, of the panaceas has any justification. While Kentucky Fried Chicken is now called KFC, the chicken is still fried, and McDonalds still asks, "You want fries with that?" And now you're even asked, "Do you want large fries with that?"

On the one hand, medical advancement may improve longevity, but that would not necessarily help to overcome general obesity as an

---

[8]P. Nelson. 2018. *UBI and the Threat to Democracy as We Know It* (New York, NY: Business Expert Press).

outcome of lack of exercise (combined with eating too much or badly), so in regard to habitats, there would need to be access to gyms or other ways to exercise. Following on the "carrot and stick" principle, advertising has to be controlled in some way (as with cigarettes) and some benefit should reward compliance (free fruit in supermarkets). Alternatively, someone might invent a system where exercising could do something useful, perhaps by having cycling machines linked to electricity generators.[9]

In habitat design, smoking has been considerably sidelined with the provision of smoking rooms, while the coverage of its prohibition has been extended. However, since governments still collect massive revenue from the sale of tobacco, its total abolition will take some time. On the other hand, tobacco smoking is likely to be gone within the next 100 years, but then perhaps people with different lifestyles will be smoking something else.

Experts predict major health problems with obesity, depending, of course, on the country involved, but for the Western world, it is broadly estimated that one in three people have some difficulty with their weight, bringing on diabetic and other issues.[10]

There are probable changes in the offing that might appear unrealistic at present, but outlandish solutions are still being demanded, for example, movements aligned with global warming crusaders calling for the culling of cattle to stop them farting and releasing methane into the atmosphere. While the introduction of such a policy appears unlikely, it could lead to larger concentrations of vegetarians, which would trigger both health issues and cost implications.

Mental

In relation to mental health, while the number of reported cases is no doubt on the rise, this might be partly because more people feel encouraged to seek help, unlike earlier when it was customary to keep problems to oneself. Estimates vary on levels of depression and are hard to verify, but figures released in the media in Australia on Mental Health

---

[9] Already tried in the United States but did not produce meaningful power.

[10] N. Fuller. 2017. *Integral Weight Loss* (London, UK: Penguin).

Day report depression affecting one in five people. This could be one of the major issues to be faced 100 years from now, but the question of what constitutes negative mental health needs close scrutiny since this can often be linked with individual expectations, and, as with the definition of "happiness," the concept is difficult to quantify.

If suicide rates are an indication of the effect of mental health problems, trying to identify lifestyles by country provides little help. What, for example, would put Sri Lanka at the head of the list with 35.3 per 100,000 suicides and Lithuania second, at 32.7?[11] Stress in South Korea arising from the need to either get ahead or suffer social stigma could explain their ranking third with 28.3 percent, but the statistics fail to explain why Belgium, with assisted suicides, comes in at 15 with a rate of 20.5 per 100,000. All of these rates could be interpreted in many ways since it would also not then explain why countries such as Afghanistan (5.5) and Iraq and Syria (2.7) have such low rates when one would not expect that they are the happiest countries in which to live. Perhaps they do not record suicides for one reason or the other? Aren't there also countries such as the Bahamas, Jamaica, and Barbados, where suicide is basically unheard of?

Equated alongside suicide rates are the world's ten happiest countries on a list of 156, led by Finland, followed by Norway, Denmark, Iceland, Switzerland, the Netherlands, Canada, New Zealand,[12] and the United States, ranked 18th (falling four spots last year owing to obesity, substance abuse, and untreated depression). Overall, citizens were asked to rank their countries on a 1–10 scale on the basis of six objectives (Cantril Ladder): health, life expectancy, social support, freedom, trust (absence of corruption), and generosity.

Since some of these ideals may be considered subjective, they could be widely interpreted but may define the lifestyle people require in future, starting with healthy life expectancy and incorporating social connectivity. Happiness otherwise appears difficult to define, given always that there is "happy happy" and "happy contented," that is, true happiness

[11]World Population Review www.worldpopulationreview.com
[12]Sixth World Happiness Report, United Nations Sustainable Development Solutions Network.

while understanding everything available against being simply reconciled to what one has.

The question of health therefore has two planning dimensions, the first providing facilities for institutionalization and treatment and the second making living conditions such as to ease the pressure on mental illness. While one can build facilities and hospitals, the prevention of mental illness is another question given that the basic extended family concept no longer exists in most societies and reduces automatic support. This can be exemplified by China's replacement of traditional Hutongs[13] by high-rise housing, where people lost their earlier social connections and, under the one-child policy, leaving one child to look after and support two family grandparents.

Humans are basically herd animals, so linkages with the herd and one's position in that structure should affect the degree of happiness. The question is whether people are benefiting from the linkage with others; is the physical side improving; and does having 5,000 followers on Facebook, LinkedIn, or Twitter encourage a feeling of connectivity if a person might personally know only a few of those people and really converse with just one or two? Will this situation improve in future, and will it contribute to herd connectivity and happiness?

Pets and Support

One of the ways physical and mental health can be maintained has long been linked to individuals owning and interfacing with pets, mainly cats and dogs. Apart from the recognizable "blind dogs," there are also now the officially recognized "support dogs" to assist in stress disorder.[14] On the one hand, dogs can be used to prompt exercise, countering obesity and related illnesses, while, on the other hand, both dogs and cats can provide emotional support, especially for people living alone.

In designing habitats for the future, the pet issue needs to be considered in regard to accommodation provided as well as determining what pets can be owned, whether they can be allowed to breed as well as to be

---

[13]Narrow streets or alleyways most common in Beijing.
[14]INVICTUS Games Sydney October 2018 provided such dogs for athletes.

sold, how they are housed, and how defecation is handled. Laws now exist on collection of dog droppings, although that in itself may not be considered hygienic, while a local council in Sydney is debating introducing a ban on cats being allowed outside.

The futuristic issue in this regard links with the emergence of robotic companions who can also talk back and hold conversations. The ultimate effect of this on mental health can only be speculated on, but an old person might be happier with a dog to talk to rather than having no one. The overall catch for 2120 is, how with all the likely new options to connect with artificial intelligence (AI), humans are able to maintain their touch with reality, and if they can't, what will be the effect?

Longevity

Other than what governments may have planned for people later in their life, while the "sanctity of life" is still recognized, proceeding on the assumption that everyone is entitled to live the best life that they can, the likelihood that the majority of humans in future will be able to live longer is borne out by historical trends.

Variation is seen from country to country; in the United States white male life expectancy for those born in 1900 was 47 years, while for those born in 2000 that figure rose by 60 percent to 75. For black men, the improvement was greater, from 33 to 68, 35 additional years, showing a 65 percent improvement.[15] Women, as always, do better.

In Africa, however, it is reported that only three countries currently have life expectancies of over 70.[16] They are Mauritius (74.82), Seychelles (73.26), and Cape Verde (73.17); South Africa's life expectancy is 63.6, and Lesotho's, at 52.94, is the lowest.

While certain areas may have some catching up to do, the overall interpretation would be that average life expectancy by 2120 will at least be over 100 years, but, of course, while this might refer to simply remaining alive rather than living an enjoyable life, it comes with limiting factors such as cognizance and physical ability.

---

[15]Senior living.org
[16]WHO Publish Data 2018.

Humans have moved a long way from the calculated life span bordering prehistory at 30 to 35, and while the achievement may be considered remarkable, those limiting early life spans could have been a result of infection and disease, which always need to be considered.[17]

On the other side of this equation is the postulate by leading scientists, including the Dean of Medicine at Harvard, George Daley,[18] that the wealthy will soon be able to clone, edit, or hack their genes for longevity and thus to create a class of super beings, which could then render the rest of the population superfluous.[19] The compromise to this was suggested as forming a body to regulate, and even outlaw, such cloning, but if the people involved were the superintelligent it is more likely that they would be the ones formulating the rules.

---

[17]Sharon Basaraba, A Guide to Longevity throughout History, from the Prehistoric Onward, June 11, 2018.

[18]International Summit on Human Genome Editing 2015.

[19]S. Hawkins. October 19, 2018. *Brief Answers to the Big Questions* (Seattle, WA: Amazon).

CHAPTER 6

Government Planning Response

Different Components

Planning theory is the body of scientific concepts, definitions, behavioral relationships, and assumptions that define the body of knowledge for urban planning. There are eight procedural theories of planning that remain the principal ones today: the rational–comprehensive approach (logical from problem identification through to solution); the incremental approach (based on everyday actual rather than planned); the transactive approach (communicative rationality), which is also the communicative approach; the advocacy approach (presenting issues from various groups); the equity approach (where urban planners work within government and use their research to influence opinion helping to redistribute public and private resources); the radical approach (equitable and community-based manner); and the humanist, phenomenological,[1] or personal approach.[2]

Actual planning has long been a combination of the different methods listed, but the trend appears to be in favor of the equity approach, which could be considered as planners attempting to provide for the interests of communities as a whole. It is likely that this will continue in future, given the interrelationships between groups. The big question will really be whether the groups in future will be interested or whether governments are in such control as to dictate in favor of expediency. This gets back to the perennial problem of whether planners can come up with ways to keep specific interest groups happy or whether these have to

---

[1]Phenomenology is the study of structures of consciousness as experienced from the first-person point of view. The central structure of an experience is its intentionality.
[2]American Society of Planning 1967.

reduce everyone to a basic common denominator. In other words, does one have to regulate in such a way as to protect the dumbest person in the community rather than assume that a normal person should know coffee served in a restaurant is likely to be hot?[3]

While these are all good planning theories, they need to be considered alongside issues such as urban planning around urban developments that already exist, as against new urban development where nothing exists so that planners have free rein to design to a model.[4] When the planning runs out of available land on which to build, are old areas leveled to start again, and what is done with the existing inhabitants during the move? What new materials are then chosen?

Materials

With future urban habitat designs, a range of building materials will be available within a wide range of costs.

In line with the hypothesis that individual living space will reduce with larger populations, designs and materials are likely to follow suit. Concrete, as the major building material to date, will likely continue for large constructions, but concrete itself will change considerably, and it has already been seen how fiberglass as one material can be used in the construction of small living spaces. This has been used in building the small live-in modules in Japan. In earthquake-prone regions such as New Zealand, wood is used for the construction of normal housing so that there is give when land vibrations strike.

Japan has had to become a global leader in high-rise earthquake-resistant development, putting whole buildings on a floating base and tying it together so that it, and not the entire building, is hit by the shock. Most governments have formulated regulations covering construction and building materials, which are to be followed in developed or developing areas. The bottom line here is that, as can be seen in many,

---

[3]There is the famous case where McDonalds was used by a customer who was burnt because the coffee was hot.
[4]Colonel William Light (1786 to 1839) designed the city of Adelaide in South Australia, recognized for its planning excellence aiming at "Good sense" and "Follow nature," but had almost a clean slate to work on.

especially Asian, new developments in China (including Hong Kong), Japan, Manila, etc., apartments are being permitted to become smaller and smaller concrete blocks and, unfortunately, this continuance is inevitable.

Around the standardized and cheapest building of these new concrete jungles, experiments continue in converting waste to bricks, and there is even 3D-printed sandstone. The question with these new systems is how their usage remains in relation to costs and what is required to house hundreds of thousands of people in a confined area. The only direction to be seen is in building small high-rise apartments but then trying to make them as livable as possible by offering modern facilities such as clothes washing and drying, microwave cooking, simplified rubbish removal, plumbing, and access to transport, all at a low purchase or rental cost.

Depending on the areas, the way buildings are constructed will include prefabrication, where whole houses come in kits to be erected on-site in a day. This will apply to normal residential housing as well as to emergency accommodation. Current versions have such modules coming with already installed electricity and plumbing.

Where a solution has yet to be found is in the provision of housing for the ever-increasing number of people living in substandard housing, in slums, or on the street. Many countries, whether developed or not, have ignored the issue as they either lack the will or the finances to address the problem or don't have available land on which to relocate people. Often when this is tried, people do not want to move because new areas do not have jobs or otherwise allow them to live off the street. Addressing this problem will possibly require a staged solution in which the willing are first moved, the remainder then placed in makeshift tent villages where the designs and materials are already available, and finally all of them moved into low-cost housing.

Connectivity

Following on from the different types of planning, the biggest problem for governments is to keep their populations "happy" or at least contented enough so that they will not rise up in sufficient numbers to take over control. Individuals vying for government leadership positions are supposed to have an altruistic reason for doing so. This is great in theory but hard to see in practice, even if Trump is taken as an example of someone who could possibly have done better remaining a businessman than vying for president with the accompanying aggravation. An ancient Greek philosopher suggested that anyone wanting the top job should have a limited tenure and then commit suicide at the end of it, thereby proving their bona fides in public service.

The issue, again, is that all planning for living in the future will bring with it further complications in connectivity as large groups of diverse individuals will be inhabiting living space in close proximity.

SWAT Analysis

In the analysis of governments' urban planning response, it's worthwhile to consider the strengths and weaknesses under current systems and roll these out into likely outcomes for future development. Within this context, however, it still remains a question of linking different cultures and countries toward a unified whole where, no matter what the differences, humans will need to live together in ever-increasing proximity.

Despite the various issues confronting different countries, leaving aside those involving the failed states, planning issues facing the central government remain similar.

Strengths

The main benefit governments have in planning responses is that in the online world they have up-to-date data on past, present, and, now, future projections to incorporate into planning models. With the information available, it is possible to determine the general consensus on population statistics in their various forms, rates of births, deaths, and so-called "marriages," while at the same time planning on how to house the inhabitants, feed them, and keep them under control.

Similarly, the access to data can help the government test what their constituents desire in their planning, having seen where public protests have turned developments around, even though not always following the most logical course.[5]

Weaknesses

The major weaknesses in all planning models hinge on the unknown population movements and possible major as well as minor political uprisings. This is coupled with the problem of models where elected politicians react to what voters might think they want and give it to them even if this is not in the voters' long-run interests. This is aligned to the planning models earlier outlined that tend toward ethical distribution of resources but remain likely skewed in the interest of individuals with wealth connected to influence. Added to this now becomes the undue influence of a few moblike decisions based on knee-jerk Twitter reactions that prompt opinion polls and political reaction.

With online real-time connectivity, politicians respond to what people believe they want as of today, and this is what politicians react to in running polls and immediate Twitter reactions to any news event. This does not, however, predict what future generations will be looking for or even whether humans themselves will have changed physically in response to diet or longevity.[6]

The biggest danger still remains the one-person–one-vote assumption under democracy that allows people to react unreasonably if given that opportunity. In the past it did not matter since policies could be put forward and debated over time. Now on the eve of a poll, totally fictitious assertions can be made, and people reacting to their social media feeds will vote in response, after which it is too late.[7] Alternatively, voters

---

[5]This is where logical and otherwise necessary major roads or tunnels in a democratic country can be halted owing to protests from small vocal and politically connected groups. Countries such as China, Russia, or Vietnam do not have these restrictions.

[6]The Times, October 20, 2018, Health Metrics and Evaluation. The Spanish will become a country of longevity by 2040, reaching 85.8, to exceed Japan despite a high smoking and drinking population.

[7]US "Presidential" election.

can be so far removed from reality as to be unable to make rational decisions.[8]

Opportunities

With the development of artificial intelligence (AI), it may be possible to improve planning to the stage where future expectations can be programmed into the planning equation. Opportunities seem almost endless, with AI able to connect and interface onto any job or activity, leading to situations inconceivable today but likely to be commonplace in 100 years' time.

Again, with improved connectivity, which is heading toward systems where physical linkages are no longer required, the ability to absorb limitless data will be increased beyond current comprehension, and supercomputers will provide access to the stars and beyond.

Threats

With so much new development and access to what will amount to almost unlimited data, many new benefits will be available that will also bring with them the dangers of information overload, making it difficult for individuals to sift useful data from the myriad sources available. In addition, it will become necessary to distinguish between information that is true and that which has been introduced for any number of purposes, whether it be promotion of commercial interests or pursuit of political aspirations. While, of course, algorithms will be developed to help sort out data validity, these programs in themselves are always subject to compromise, so there could be a situation where everything is available but it is difficult to know what to use. The outcome of this is that individuals no longer know what is real and what is not and so are able to be led, either by altruistic governments or their opposite. Individuals could become indifferent or unresponsive, abrogating their right to contribute

---

[8]In the U.S. November 2018 mid-term elections, Dennis Hof, a brothel owner, was elected although having died in October. Mel Carnahan back in 2000 was also elected to the Senate despite having been dead for 3 weeks.

to the decision making in their own interests, or failing to be able to even determine what those interests are.

The next biggest threat to an acceptable urban planning response then becomes one where the global world order falls into the hands of a single autocratic government that rules on what it believes is best for the population or species as a whole, while the rest have to simply accept this.[9] While this may be suitable where that ruler is altruistic, the "what if" becomes whether that controlling entity decides social engineering has to kick in, certain sections of the population need to be aborted, old people euthanized, and anyone considered breaking a decreed law, no matter how trivial and without due process, is executed.

---

[9]P. Nelson. 2018. *UBI and the Threat to Democracy as We Know It* (New York, NY: Business Expert Press).

CHAPTER 7

Biological Risk Assessment

Natural Progression

The close proximity and interaction with other people accompanying the increase in the world's population greatly increases the risk of cross contamination should biological problems occur. There have been recent outbreaks of diseases such as the Ebola virus in West Africa, and while this was contained, it did cost many lives and demonstrated how very quickly such an infection could spread across the globe. Major outbreaks of disease have also occurred in China, but with the ability of the authorities to keep this under the radar, even outbreaks of bird flu were made public only long after the problem emerged. One must also remember the massive impact of the bubonic plague caused in that instance by rats, which was said to have taken out the aforementioned 33 percent of the then known Western population.

The closer proximity of urban developments in future will also affect the interaction of viruses and disease; a recent study has revealed that flu in big cities has longer seasons, while in small cities the experience is more intense.[1]

The bottom line is that the risk is very real, raising the need to consider the implications in relation to urban planning involving control of hygiene, rubbish disposal, ducting of clean air, and provision of fresh water.

---

[1] B.D. Dalziel, S. Kissler, J.R. Gog, C. Viboud, O.N. Bjørnstad, C.J.E. Metcalf, and B.T. Grenfell. October 5, 2018. "Urbanization and Humidity Shape the Intensity of Influenza Epidemics in U.S. Cities," *Science* 362, no. 6410, pp. 75–79, doi: 10.1126/science.aat6030

Atmosphere

The current new generation might find it difficult to comprehend that the air pollution witnessed at its worst during the Great Smog of London in December 1952, in the last century, was said to kill over 6,000 people and make ill more than 100,000. The fact that the smog dispersed as soon as the weather changed is little comfort on a planetary scale if it is considered that the pollution had to have moved somewhere else.

It was said that with the London situation cold weather preceding the smog prompted more people to burn coal for heating. This produced smoke from nearby coal-fired power stations at Fulham, Battersea, Bankside, Greenwich, and Kingston on Thames, producing sulphur dioxide, causing the illness and then deaths. While this was an extreme example, in Beijing as late as 2000 the low-quality sulphur coal used for power generation would leave cars daubed with orange spots during winter when it rained.[2] Similarly, smog and low air quality in other parts of China (and Hong Kong), India, Bangladesh, Vietnam, etc. cause considerable health issues, and individuals in some areas have already resorted to wearing cloth masks on the street and even employing forms of gas masks.

From that UK wake-up call and the Clean Air Act that followed the London smog, the situation in London is much better today and the air issue has been recognized elsewhere. Nevertheless, attention was raised, but it should not be forgotten how some unforeseen eventuality can arise that might not always have as simple a solution as a weather change. Consequently, factory pollution needs to be moved away from urban areas, and, in any event, the emissions need to be curtailed with the latest technology.

Ocean Degradation

The oceans have received less careful environmental attention despite their size, five oceans constituting 71 percent of the earth's surface area, so urban planning needs to take notice of what is required to keep and sustain our oceans. The main focus of these, apart from the obvious control

---

[2]This was the author's personal observation while living in Beijing.

over marine life contributing to food, is a serious situation in regard to the effect on ocean temperatures, resulting in what can now be seen as climate changes.

Oceanographers have predicted how global warming can affect the various ocean streams that could change their direction in future and therefore largely affect the weather patterns as they are currently understood. What this means in urban planning is that past plans have been designed to meet weather patterns as they are now understood but could require a totally different approach in an unknown future, with the issue moving to global cooling rather than warming as current ocean streams change direction. Different low-lying areas previously not at risk could become threatened. The question here, again, is simply the time frame in which it is possible to respond.

The urban planning side of this problem is to design structures for living that reduce and aim to eliminate ocean pollution, which could in some quarters be said to have reached endemic levels. Obviously, education is a forerunner in this equation, but how waste can be disposed of is a significant issue that urban designers need to address.[3]

Plastics

Plastics in the world's oceans have been identified as one of the major challenges for the future. Some claims, although difficult to substantiate, have been made to the effect that by 2050 there will be more plastic in the ocean than fish.[4] While this might be considered an extreme prediction, given that it is impossible to count fish in the ocean, the fatal effects of plastics on turtles and other marine life have received much publicity, and it is generally agreed that this buildup of plastic cannot continue.

From the urban planning perspective, the challenge is simply how to first prevent these contaminants from getting into the oceans and, once in, how to get them out. On land, there remains the need to dispose of the plastic in some suitable manner.

---

[3]See Super Cities and the Korean example of tubular waste disposal.
[4]Ellen Macarthur Foundation, *The New Plastic Economy.*

Of equal importance is that a chemical, bisphenol, found in everyday plastic items could lead to a six-fold increase in premature babies.[5] Similarly, phthalates found in packaging material have been found to double the risk of early birth in women.

One of the current problems concerning not just plastics but handling of rubbish, in general, is the political agenda against any considered global warming outcome, and while, on the one hand, environmental supporters want to recycle it, they block the means by which to do so on the other.[6]

Desalination

With so many people on the planet and their numbers constantly increasing, it is necessary to think ahead in all urban planning. While the availability of fresh drinking water is a risk issue for the future that is currently being addressed by the use of desalination plants, recent scientific attention has been directed at the effect desalination can have on the oceans in general. There is a concern that while there are vast areas of ocean, removing the salt from seawater and pumping it back can considerably increase the salinity of the ocean and put marine life at risk. Consequently, for every solution side effects need to be considered.

Barbiturates

While it might appear a lesser issue in regard to a biological risk, drugs and their self-induced inappropriate use present a serious global threat.

On the one hand, drug use has become endemic in some societies, while in other places such as California and Canada, cannabis has been made legal and is not seen as a threat. This does, however, appear in some eyes to pose a health risk, as anyone who has ever been in a car driven by someone high after smoking weed would readily admit.

---

[5]Daily Telegraph, Sydney, October 10, 2018.
[6]Sydney NSW recently blocked a recycling furnace electricity generator that was certified as pollution free.

There is also the additional problem that with more time for leisure in future, or at least more free time through job loss, drug taking will increase as a substitute for work and society, or large parts of it, could simply become addicted.

Pandemic

The big question is to identify what sort of pandemic could hit the globe and what planning national and international bodies can do to, first, preempt and, second, respond to the threats. The good news here is that global issues bring countries together. Orson Welles, in his *War of the Worlds*, postulated that an attack from Mars would at least bring all governments together, and this has largely been proven correct in relation to recent earthquakes and tsunamis, yet the question that remains is what countries will do if something strikes on a global scale and, logically, where self-interest would have individual governments looking after themselves first. An example would be where the required vaccinations would not be available in sufficient amounts for everyone, a situation that would be exacerbated if costs limited treatment to those who can afford it.

Back to urban planning responses, governments need to be able to contain certain areas to stop people movement as soon as they have warning and to do this quickly. This means locking down airports, shipping, and roads, the latter not being easy to do. In many countries, "heat" cameras have already been installed at airports, checking arriving passengers for possible illness.

While contaminations might be caused by new viruses, countries should be able to store some common likely medication as antidotes for first action response and have isolation buildings available for any disaster response.

CHAPTER 8

Disaster Response Mechanisms

Global

On a global basis, the World Health Organization (WHO) is designed to monitor disease and plan global controls and response along with the Centre for Disease Control (CDC), which has a similar function. Other than on these health issues there exists no central globally recognized response organization, and so calamities are usually handled by local governments on the spot with whatever support they are able to obtain from other countries.[1]

There exist agencies such as the Global Emergency Response Coalition, a lifesaving humanitarian alliance formed in 2017, made up of eight of the world's largest United States–based international aid organizations, whose goal is to work collectively to deliver relief to millions of children and families in need. However, it provides services related to general assistance rather than as part of a response unit. There are other international response agencies such as Catholic Aids Response Effort (CARE), Congregations around Richmond Involved to Assure Shelter (Caritas), the Red Cross, and Doctors Without Borders as well as other organizations concerned with halting problems related to human and drug trafficking, but countries hit by major calamities must rely on the nearest and most appropriate form of assistance.

---

[1]This is not always true when some countries feel they are abrogating control and wish to control the issue themselves.

Civilian Uprising

The question, no matter how unpalatable, that still needs to be asked in relation to urban planning is, what needs to be built in during an instance of uprising? The simplest example is the situation where countries want to protect their borders from illegal immigrants and have to grapple with the difficult points and how one handles possible country entry points such as the *Chunnel* or where a river acts as a border between two countries.

What need to be considered here are the physical fortifications and the provision of facilities to handle any transgressors. Examples are the Australian policy stipulations that no illegal immigrants are to reach Australian shores, and hence if any are intercepted they are to be arrested and relocated in offshore detention centers as a dissuasive measure. Similar are recent issues on the unpopular measure of separating children from their families on illegal entry into the United States. These are diverse political issues that still involve planning in regard to handling integration.

On a local planning level, part of what is required is for authorities to be able to lock down entry points and even whole suburbs to contain disturbances allowing access only to police and emergency vehicles. One way police do this is by breaking up demonstrations by switching traffic lights in short breaks to red to break up processions and then arresting people crossing on the red.

Biological

Within overall development planning, there needs to be a biological response mechanism built in on various levels. As with the Ebola out-break in the not too distant past, there needs to be a way to contain this locally, quarantine the country, and advise other countries of possible transmissions.

Beyond the immediate reaction, medicines need to be kept ready for delivery as an immediate response to any known disease outbreak and the capability to identify new strains of viruses or completely new diseases should be in place. As demonstrated recently, at times there aren't enough batches of medicines available to go around, which brings us back to the issue that if there is a problem on a global basis and a shortage of vaccines, the countries in a dominant position will safeguard their interests first, leaving open the question about what becomes of the rest. Where the earth still has large areas of slums and primitive conditions of hygiene and sanitary services, disease is a major threat, which is only increased by ease of global movement.

Within all of the standard responses is the need to examine how diseases or infections not yet identified are to be handled. One need only recall how HIV/AIDS took the world by surprise and how long it took to respond to the issue.

Drugs

As part of the attempt to counter or curtail the side effects of habitual self-imposed drug use, some communities have responded by supplying less addictive drug substitutes and in other cases have provided user rooms, in which sterile needles are provided to reduce the incidence of cross infection.

Overshadowing the overall complicated issue of drugs is the question of whether governments have given up fighting what is seen as a losing battle, trying overall prevention and experimenting with legalization instead and looking at whether reducing the amount of money in illegal distribution could minimize the problem. It is difficult to see how legalizing cannabis would not induce individuals to try something stronger, although filling up jails with small-time users and dealers would not be cost effective. Hence, under urban planning some redesign of the penal system should become a priority so that once jailed, this does not impose limitations on future prospects, since the world does not need millions of offenders as another underclass to be catered to. In this it is pointless to pretend that after having been jailed and tagged with a criminal record, this does not taint an offender for life, making it likely they would offend again.

Global Warming Consequences

The predicted threat of global warming and the associated response mechanisms have been built into most country plans. Calamities such as tsunamis, landslides, or building collapses have been seen to evoke immediate reactions while they remain in the public eye. However, as the emergency passes, interest dies, as illustrated by Haiti, where, long after the latest disaster, people are still living in makeshift shacks.

The major initial concern when responding to global warming issues is in regard to what is perceived as sea level rises with two main consequences: people living in low-lying areas around river deltas that become swamped on a regular basis but where they can at least move to higher ground, to islands that are already only slightly above water.

Where there is danger of populations being swamped, such as on islands like Tuvalu, the population has largely managed to obtain New Zealand residency in emergencies and currently has more immediate problems of being inundated with rubbish they cannot dispose of. The real question becomes, what is the actual level of rising seas and what is the time frame?

Less difficult to predict is the validity of the hypothesis that *global warming* will in the longer term lead to *global cooling* and a return to an ice age. These projections come from the climate change affecting the earth's sensitive ocean currents, which for now have cooling effects that could change. Time frames for this, however, seem to extend well beyond the next hundred years.

Space Debris

Bearing the fate of the dinosaurs in mind, we can say that the earth could still be in danger of catastrophic damage from outer space. To date, scientists appear to have this issue covered with their tracking systems, but only recently an asteroid appeared to have slipped by their early warning alarms.

Consequently, as a protective measure in planning, governments need to keep upgrading their monitoring systems while at the same time developing a response to a scenario should one of these space objects be predicted to be on a trajectory toward earth. No such plan is yet known to exist, although experiments are afoot to land rockets on large asteroids in an effort to change their trajectories away from earth.

Country Specific

For global planning on disaster response, developed countries still need to ensure vaccines are available where recently even flu vaccines have run short. Developed countries are likely to be ahead of undeveloped countries in this area, so to ensure that a countrywide outbreak is contained, planning should look at global stocks that could be delivered rapidly to any required area.

The cost of centralized supply should be internationally funded to avert a pandemic should one ever arise.

Local

When local supplies are being planned, a margin should be provided just above average expected usage. Where countries cannot afford to store vaccines, they should be assisted, in the interest of the world as a whole, given the speed at which infection has been observed to travel.

One of the most critical issues in formulating a disaster response is to have a plan and have this publicized so that the people in authority are aware of it and can access it, ensuring that it clearly identifies the people who are at various levels of authority.[2]

---

[2]Japanese fishing vessel Nissan Maru No. 8 sank off the southern Tasmanian coast in 1976, with the loss of 21 lives, the day of the Hobart Cup horse race, where all emergency responders were at races and unable to call out emergency response. The police commissioner was only advised four hours after the report was phoned in.

CHAPTER 9

Legal Framework

Governance

A great deal has been written on good governance in regard to urban planning, such as the need to promote good urban governance by strengthening the capacity of the authorities at all levels of government in integrated planning and public finance management, by establishing adequate legal and policy frameworks, by fostering access to public and private investments by municipalities, and by fostering women's empowerment in urban governance matters. These are all great aspirations, provided they can be acted upon.

Where planning legislation is enacted, it needs to be followed through in the legal system. An outstanding example of this would be the famed tourist island of Boracay in the Philippines, which became so popular and crowded that buildings were going up with little consideration for planning permits, and sewage was running into the sea. Here was a case of rapid overdevelopment that finally could not be sustained on the basis of health and every other consideration. The mayor eventually shut down the whole island and issued subpoenas to anyone having built without approval or against the regulations, and as a result, from 2017 onward whole buildings and hotels had to be pulled down. This had to be done because the problem had become so monumental it could not be sustained, and it was calculated that, in any event, the island was so famous that tourism would continue after the rebuild. The island was reopened in October 2018.

A problem is experienced where under centrally controlled governments the designer and builder are the same as the controlling agency, and unless someone specifically complains at a sufficiently high political level no changes are going to be made. The polluting factory generating employment and returning funds for the government owning it is most unlikely to be shut down simply because a government environmental authority will complain. The only time this appears to happen is, as in the case of Boracay, when the issue hits the international press and puts the brakes on tourism in general.

International Agreements

Most of the international urban planning agreements have recently focused around climate change, global warming, its effects and the means by which to compensate and overcome it. These issues were brought to a general public focus, prompted by Al Gore's 2006 Oscar-winning Documentary *An inconvenient truth.* Gore rounds off his apocalyptic narrative with a call to action along with a list of things people can do to alleviate the situation. On the political side, he called for endorsement of the Kyoto Treaty, which led to the Paris Agreement (which, however, the major polluters have rejected).

To some extent Gore's predictions have come about, but, unfortunately, to prove the case, allegations have become confused with statistics that are difficult to link to man-made climate change. Similarly, there is a difficulty with the otherwise good all-encompassing catchphrase *CLIMATE CHANGE,* when climate has always been changing.

The call to arms has, however, been heard around the world, and while America, China, and India, as major contributors to the carbon footprint, have not acknowledged that all countries should get together to attain a target on reduction, rejecting the Paris Agreement, international support has continued in this direction. As an example, the majority of sponsored development projects from international development agencies such as The World Bank or Asian Development Bank now have a greening or "climate change" focus, and universities are turning out experts[1] in rapidly increasing numbers. A large part of the development assistance is therefore focused on guarding urban habitats against increased storms, flooding, sea rises, and species extinction along with rising temperatures

---

[1]Many of these posts call for at least 10 years' experience, although these posts did not exist in the past.

predicted to increase death tolls for the elderly. The main problem remains that a great deal of this assistance to countries in the formulation of their urban development strategies requires concentration of plans on "greening" public spaces and reduction of their carbon footprint, something that is difficult for developing countries to understand while they still have large populations living in mud huts and shacks wiped out by annual floods.

International Agencies

The core of the encompassing climate change issue can be seen within the United Nations Conference on Housing and Sustainable Urban Development (Habitat III).[2] Other involvement and support comes from:

- African Development Bank (AfDB)
- Asian Development Bank (ADB)
- Asian Infrastructure Investment Bank (AIIB)
- Caribbean Development Bank (CDB)
- Colombo Plan (CP)
- Development Bank of Latin America (CAF)
- European Bank for Reconstruction and Development (EBRD)
- European Investment Bank
- Food and Agriculture Organization of the United Nations (FAO)
- Inter-American Development Bank (IADB)
- International Bank for Reconstruction and Development (IBRD–World Bank Group)
- International Development Law Organization (IDLO)
- International Fund for Agricultural Development (IFAD)
- International Labor Organization (ILO)
- International Monetary Fund (IMF)
- International Organization for Migration (IOM)
- International Red Cross (ICRC AND IFRC)

---

[2]UN-Habitat (2017) action agenda to be taken in five areas: (i) National urban policies, (ii) Urban legislation, rules and regulations, (iii) Urban planning and design, (iv) Urban economy and municipal finance, and (v) Local implementation.

- Islamic Development Bank (IDB)
- Multilateral Investment Guarantee Agency (MIGA, part of the World Bank Group)
- Organization for Economic Co-operation and Development (OECD)
- Technical Centre for Agricultural and Rural Cooperation ACP-EU (CTA)
- United Nations (UN)
- United Nations Children's Fund (UNICEF)
- United Nations Conference on Trade and Development (UNCTAD)
- United Nations Development Programme (UNDP)
- United Nations Population Fund (UNFPA)
- United Nations Environment Programme (UNEP)
- United Nations High Commissioner for Refugees (UNHCR)
- United Nations Industrial Development Organization (UNIDO)
- United Nations Office for the Coordination of Humanitarian Affairs (OCHA)
- World Bank Group
- World Food Programme (WFP)
- World Health Organization (WHO)
- World Trade Organization (WTO)

Bilateral Development Agencies

- Austrian Development Cooperation (ADC—Austrian)
- Association Francaise des Docteurs en Droit (AFdD—France)
- Canadian International Development Agency (CIDA—Canadian)
- Department for International Development (DFID—Australia)
- Department For International Development Cooperation (DFIDC—Finland)
- Department of Foreign Affairs and Trade (DfAT—UK)
- Danish International Development Agency (DANIDA—Denmark)
- German Development Agency (GIZ—Germany)
- Directorate for International Development Cooperation (ICEIDA—Iceland)
- Japanese International Cooperation Agency (JICA—Japan)
- Norwegian Agency For Development (NORAD—Norway)
- Swedish International Development Agency (SIDA—Sweden)

- China International development Cooperation (SIDCA—China)
- United States Agency for International Development (USAID—USA)

These are additionally supported directly by the interventions of the ministry of foreign affairs in various countries.

Other Agencies

These include the following:

- U.S. Environmental Impact Agency
- Urban Climate Change Resilience Trust Fund (UCCRTF) and the Global Environment Facility (GEF)
- U.S. Green Building Council (USGBC) Leadership in Energy and Environmental Design (LEED), one of the most popular green building certification programs used worldwide. Developed by the nonprofit U.S. Green Building Council (USGBC), it includes a set of rating systems for the design, construction, operation, and maintenance of green buildings, homes, and neighborhoods that aim to help building owners and operators be environmentally responsible and use resources efficiently.
- Earth System Governance Project (ESGP)
- Global Green Growth Institute (GGGI)
- Intergovernmental Panel on Climate Change (IPCC)
- International Union for Conservation of Nature (IUCN)
- United Nations Environment Programme (UNEP)
- European Environment Agency (EEA)
- Partnerships in Environmental Management for the Seas of East Asia (PEMSEA).

In addition to these agencies, they are supported by others linked specifically to disaster relief of one kind or another, including the World Health Organization and the Center for Disease Control and Prevention (CDC).

These agencies in turn are linked with the support of Habitat for Humanity offering a central focus on the overall concept, remembering also that, by definition,[3] habitats change over time. Such change may be

---

[3]Wikipedia observation on habitat.

due to violent events, including a volcanic eruption, an earthquake, a tsunami, a wildfire, or a change in oceanic currents; or the change may be more gradual, over millennia, with alterations in the climate, as ice sheets and glaciers advance and retreat and as different weather patterns bring changes in precipitation and solar radiation. Other changes come as a direct result of human activities, such as deforestation, the ploughing of ancient grasslands, the diversion and damming of rivers, the draining of marshland, and the dredging of the seabed. Consequently, urban planning needs to look ahead and try to preempt these changes.

There is no attempt to deal here with all of the agencies supporting approaches to future urban development, since these can easily be looked up; suffice it to note that there are many of them, all of which have *climate change* interests.

The 2030 Agenda for Sustainable Development, adopted by all United Nations Member States in 2015, provides a shared blueprint for peace and prosperity for people and the planet, now and into the future with 17 sustainable development goals (SDGs), which are an urgent call for action by all countries in a global partnership. Again, they recognize that ending poverty and other deprivations must go hand in hand with strategies that improve health and education, reduce inequality, and spur economic growth, all while tackling climate change and working to preserve oceans and forests.[4] This initiative led to the following:

- In June 1992, at the Earth Summit in Rio de Janeiro, Brazil, more than 178 countries adopted Agenda 21, which was a comprehensive plan of action to build a global partnership for sustainable development to improve human lives and protect the environment.
- Member States unanimously adopted the Millennium Declaration at the Millennium Summit in September 2000 at UN Headquarters in New York. The summit led to the elaboration of eight millennium development goals (MDGs) to reduce extreme poverty by 2015.
- The Johannesburg Declaration on Sustainable Development and the Plan of Implementation, adopted at the Development in South

---

[4]UN Sustainable Development Goals, Knowledge Platform.

Africa in 2002, reaffirmed the global community's commitments to poverty eradication and the environment and built on Agenda 21 and the Millennium Declaration by laying greater emphasis on multilateral partnerships.

- At the United Nations Conference on Sustainable Development (Rio+20) in Rio de Janeiro, Brazil, in June 2012, Member States adopted the outcome document "The future we want," in which they decided, inter alia, to launch a process to develop a set of SDGs to build upon the MDGs and to establish the UN High-level Political Forum on Sustainable Development. The Rio +20 outcome also contained other measures for implementing sustainable development, including mandates for future programs of work in development financing and small island developing states.
- In 2013, the General Assembly set up a 30-member Open Working Group to develop a proposal on the SDGs.
- In January 2015, the General Assembly began the process of negotiations on the post-2015 development agenda. The process culminated in the subsequent adoption of the 2030 Agenda for Sustainable Development, with 17 SDGs at its core, at the UN Sustainable Development Summit in September 2015.
- 2015 was a landmark year for multilateralism and international policy shaping, with the adoption of several major agreements:
  - Sendai Framework for Disaster Risk Reduction (March 2015)
  - Addis Ababa Action Agenda on Financing for Development (July 2015)
  - Transforming our world: the 2030 Agenda for Sustainable Development with its 17 SDGs was adopted at the UN Sustainable Development Summit in New York in September 2015.
  - Paris Agreement on Climate Change (December 2015)

Currently, the annual High-level Forum on Sustainable Development serves as the central UN platform for the follow-up and review of the SDGs, but, as noted, although this rhetoric is reassuring, there is little commitment from many, including the world's largest polluters, all of whom are pressing ahead with building more coal-fired power stations.

National Controls

While in the first world countries it might be a simple matter to institute controls, in the developing world, although planning might be legislated, its implementation can be another matter. This is particularly so when the government is the planning, implementation, and oversight body.[5] It also becomes a contest between governments wanting what they see as progress against restrictions that might slow this down.

The overall problem always returns to financing and development priorities. The financial model links to a multitude of objectives, many, if not all, of which have some political connotations, whereas in politics, it is never possible to please everyone. The central aim of the global bodies is to set agendas to which they can seek national agreement in return for expensive compliance funding and induce countries to tow the international line. Again, it remains much too difficult to go beyond lip service and wanting the money for impoverished countries to be talking about reducing the carbon footprint while they still have part of the population in poverty living in mud huts or slums.

Certifications

Since a number of support agencies are associated with the new science of global warming, there has been a move to bring in certifications; for example, the LEED certification program for the design, construction, and operation of high-performance green buildings was set up in 2002. This mark of excellence has international repute, and there are four levels with 100 possible base points distributed across five major credit categories, including sustainable sites, water efficiency, energy and atmosphere, materials and resources, indoor environmental quality, plus an additional six points for innovation in design and an additional four points for regional priority. LEED is not a standard but an evaluation grid attempting to offer future development projections.

While these certification exercises are helpful in defining future direction, the hypothesis remains that what is thought to be the current desire

---

[5]Vietnam Daily News highlighted that planning permits were simply ignored and major apartments built without permits, September 22, 2017.

and aspirations of future generations may turn out to be different from what they need by the time they get there.

Nevertheless, it is incumbent on the larger economies, particularly the polluters, to demonstrate some lead and contribute to the funding equation. Toward this end, China announced the establishment, in April 2018, of the State International Development Cooperation Agency (SIDCA), headed by Wang Xiaotao, the former deputy director of the National Development and Reform Commission, from 2014, where he had been specifically tasked with the responsibility for foreign capital, overseas investment, and trade. He is expected to maintain SIDCA's focus on existing regions that its aid program supports, particularly in Africa and Asia. Greater trilateral partnerships between China, a traditional donor country, and a developing country will expand under the guidance of the agency.

CHAPTER 10

Road Maps

Balancing Alternatives

As with most other aspects of urban planning, everything ultimately always comes down to the funding. When talking funding, this introduces the time factor and in turn reverts to those making the cost allocations. All of these decisions then revolve around priorities and what governs them in a cost–benefit exercise. Unfortunately, the balance is largely dependent on the political factor, where "the squeaky wheel usually gets the most oil." The rich are expected to be able to look after themselves but do not want to be inconvenienced by the less rich, and demands are made to get street kids away from harassing motorists at intersections. These laws can similarly be relaxed by saying cars do not have to stop at red lights after dark to prevent carjackings.[1]

Objectives, however, get back to those aspirations embodied in the UN millennium goals, even if these aspirations were unlikely to be achieved in their entirety. Although a good starting point, these objectives need to be broken up into individual components and, unfortunately, equated against an individual country's tax base to at least demonstrate political awareness. This, of course, becomes extremely difficult where the superrich, as a global minority, might not mind parting with some of their wealth in the cause of the unfortunate, but as the percentage level of wealth decreases in the demographic profile, there is more apprehension over how much workers are happy to be taxed to provide benefits for the nonworkers or less fortunate. On the other hand, there remains the reality that governments have to provide something for the unemployed or destitute to keep their numbers from clogging up rational development.

---

[1] As in Kenya, brought in first at Westlake in Nairobi.

An urban development roadmap therefore has to consider all the levels of demographic planning, including degree of separation as well as connectivity, in order to meet geographical aspirations. While this is a difficult task, it is at least simplified when planning is restricted to one country or one political system.

International Connectivity

Planning roadmaps for urban development on a global scale between countries depends largely on individual political systems having to interface as well as on many other important factors. A current part of this equation is still related to countries following strict religious beliefs that depict how governments can address planning and its enforcement. In the Philippines, for example, with an estimated 98 percent Christian following, the population can reasonably be controlled through fatalism and the idea that whatever happens might be God's will, and, similarly, in Saudi Arabia God can also be held accountable.

Disparities between countries and living conditions will influence the desire to move to other countries, but in most cases the instilled religious beliefs accompany the individuals. For centuries this has been a development factor, with the Western Christian ethos resulting in building of churches with the word spread around the world by evangelical missionaries. Similarly, Islam has been permeating other parts of the world as people escape from the tyranny of their own culture yet still carry its foundation with them to proliferate in other societies. It is logical that this proliferation will continue, especially under religions that allow no challenge.

Movement between different cultures and religions to other countries has resulted in the formation of enclaves where people live their traditional lives incorporating customs governing dress, food, and worship, setting up the need for local adjustment. In the overall planning context there is the requirement for the locals of a new community to have their mosques along with their halal foods and acceptance of dressing preferences. Often this does not go down well with the long-term residents in a community, but planning laws should at least be fair in what the bulk of residents might require. This usually manifests itself in the election of minorities to government.

Looking ahead, then, one may ask whether as populations are required to live in close proximity, they will assimilate or whether the enclaves will continue to proliferate, forming countries of separate tribes. This question assumes importance in relation to the types of cities and urban habitats designed in current times for people who have to live in them 100 years from now.

CHAPTER 11

Designer Cities

Components

Now

What do people of the present, and the upcoming teenage generation, expect from their cities and habitats when they grow to adulthood? In the first instance, one would assume the governing factor in response to this question would be how well-off generations X, Y, and Z see themselves in particular countries, with the less advantaged considering movement in the advanced direction, wanting what they see available in the West.

An interesting phenomenon that has managed to equalize how well off these teenagers see themselves has come from the use of the Internet, where access to computers and phones gives younger people the possibility of communicating and playing games beyond socioeconomic boundaries. This equality is highlighted by numerous media photos of arriving refugees stepping out of boats intent on looking at their iPhones.

A Nielsen Company report (2018) reveals that adults in the United States devoted about 10 hours and 39 minutes each day to consuming media during the first quarter of this year. The report concluded that out of 168 hours in a week, if more than 50 hours is spent on devices, people still need 40 hours of sleep and for all personal care such as eating, bathing, dressing, preparing food, estimated to require 3 hours a day, this then leaving 58 hours a week in all for everything else. And that 10 hours 39 minutes a day was just an average for media. Another study for 2018 by eMarketer[1] said that U.S. adults spent an average of three and a half hours on mobile devices a day, two-thirds of it on mobile phones.

---

[1] www.Emarketer.com

Obviously, such an equalizing medium as this attention to device use can be seen as a unifying human concept, but this will need to be balanced carefully against the danger of drifting into a society where reliance on these devices takes over normal human interaction and develops a life of its own.

The 2120 Vision

Looking forward over 100 years, the same question could be asked for that year's generation in 2120: What would the upcoming teenage generation then expect from their cities and habitats when they grow to adulthood?

Having recognized how through the use of devices and mobile phones this has introduced equality between both rich and poor in relation to access to information, we might see it continue in future. While it would appear certain that the IT and AI trend reliance will continue, the time will come when those with better access to training and money to acquire expertise will move to a position where they are designing the games and systems that other people are using. Nevertheless, it has been seen that level playing fields can be established where very bright young people in India have been making major leaps forward in coding and IT skills, which will give them an economic advantage for their future.

Trying to then look at what an average person might be looking for in their urban habitat a hundred years from now, it's likely that space requirements will narrow, and while some people might be able to live in mini mansions, the norm is likely to be contained in high-tech habitats, providing an individual base from which people can interface with other humans and interact with their environmental surroundings. In the design of these habitats, following global trends, where fewer people are getting married and doing so later, living requirements are likely to require less space, and people will very likely on an average day be conferring and interacting with artificial intelligence rather than with actual humans.

The existing concepts of Siri and Google complying with commands is certain to be expanded beyond current comprehension to the extent that people will be conversing with their possibly implanted devices as part of their day-to-day existence; so the linkages with the systems will be most important.

Without going through them all individually, suffice it to note that it is possible to envisage someone being woken by the system in the morning, a robot being told to prepare breakfast, instructions passed on what groceries should be ordered and delivered during the day, quick inputs of the daily news, a rundown of the agenda for the day, a synopsis of what humans may have called during the night, questions on where to book for lunch and dinner, discussion on likely shows to see, either live or on a device that night, and then ordering a transport vehicle to go to the next daily appointment. This would be an outline for an individual living alone conversing and interacting with a "device," and it can be easily seen how this could interface with a couple or even a family. It is also easy to see how the move to a digital world becomes an easy transition that can raise all sorts of dangers of people being isolated from reality. Although a long way off, sci-fi movies such as *Total Recall* [2] have suggested the possibility of living out journeys around the world and experiencing adventures mentally rather than in reality. This can also have a detrimental effect with video games, where young people become desensitized and dissociated from reality, as in situations where the fun is crashing cars and shooting people.

On another contrived reality interface beyond the mental implants suggested is now the production of robots designed for any number of uses, including companionship. This further compromises the human interface with reality, about which many reports have come out about people forming personal relationships with their robot companions, while one man in Japan was reported as having married his robot companion.

The suggestion is that people will be able to experience "life" without actually having to take part in its reality, giving rise to the danger that the fictitious will eventually overwhelm concepts of normal life and to the question whether, in regard to habitation, the need for human companionship itself can become inconsequential.

Green

Attempting to define a green city,[3] in the era of global warming, becomes complicated since the term has become a catchphrase to be dedicated

---

[2] Arnold Schwarzenegger 1990, then Colin Farrell 2012.

[3] Engineering UTEP www.engineering.utep.edu Green City.

to increasing the compatibility of cities with their local natural systems by providing resources to link individuals and groups with each other and community-based ecological activities. The suggestion moves one to consider *ecological activities,* which include a wide range of issues covering the use and conservation of resources, reduction of the carbon footprint, recycling, and reduction of pollution. It also takes the definition on into *sustainable.*

Sustainable

A sustainable city is one designed with consideration for the social, economic, and environmental impact and resilient habitats for existing populations without compromising the ability of future generations to experience the same.[4]

Sustainable cities, under the definition, are also called eco cities.[5] These are cities inhabited by people dedicated to the goal of minimizing the required inputs of energy, water, food, waste, output of heat, minimizing pollution, CO_2, methane, and water pollution. These cities should be *ecological* or *eco-friendly.*

Unfortunately, the same composite structure creates further problems, as in the simple matter of washing and drying clothes, having to choose between power on clothes dryers and hanging unsightly washing on the balcony. The same governments that insist on saving electricity enforce the use of clothes dryers in apartment buildings.

Ecological

The design of ecological cities is sometimes referred to as *industrial ecology,* yet no agreed term exists for what a sustainable or ecological city should be. While it should meet the needs of the present without sacrificing the ability of future generations to determine their own needs, as has been postulated in this text, it is difficult to anticipate those future needs

---

[4]Wikipedia definition.
[5]R. Register. 1987. *Ecocity Berkeley: Building Cities for a Healthy Future* (Berkeley, CA: North Atlantic Books).

given that the first commercial flight was operated only in 1914, just over 100 years ago.[6] In another 100 will there be regular flights to Mars? If so, living will be in more compact units and seen as natural, not just on Mars but elsewhere too.

Compact

The compact city, or city of short distances, is an urban planning and urban design concept that promotes relatively high residential density with mixed land uses. As illustrated in the South Korean model compact city of Songdo, such a design is around a central park where anyone should be able to walk to work within 20 minutes, dispensing with the need for cars. Everything is electronically linked, and rubbish is collected through tubes to a central recycling plant.

Songdo (Island of Pine Trees) is built on tidal flats, 64 km from Seoul within the Incheon Free Economic Zone (IFEZ).[7] It is connected to Incheon International Airport by a 12-km bridge, giving it a strategic location in the Northeast Asian trading hub, from where residents could get on a plane and reach one-third of the world's population within three and a half hours.

The International Business District is conceptualized as the ultimate smart and sustainable city and a testing ground for leading-edge technological infrastructure by Cisco Systems,[8] where all dimensions of life are integrated in real estate, utilities, transportation, education, health, and government. Technically, anyone living and working within this compact city should not have to go anywhere outside for any of their needs, and everything is electronically linked, including schoolchildren, who have been fitted with microchipped bracelets in the interests of their safety.[9]

---

[6]St. Petersburg Tampa. Florida Airboat Line.

[7]The US$40 billion project is a joint venture between the City of Incheon, Gale International (61 percent), POSCO E&C (30 percent), and Morgan Stanley Real Estate (9 percent) with the Asia Development Institute, Arup & Partners, and CISCO Services Korea.

[8]Cisco revamped its Technology organization in 2007, now leader in new city technology solutions.

[9]Individuals working there report to the author that the city lacks personality.

In practice, construction of a smart city means the construction of four layers—a sensor layer, network layer, platform layer, and an application layer. While discussions by and large present the definition, vision, and characteristics of a smart city, scarcely any research has tackled what really makes cities smart.[10] The idea of smart appears linked to a technology connection at present rather than to a model designed to cater to everyone.

A further experimental so-called smart city is Nanhui New City, in the Pudong New Area, 30 km out of Shanghai (60 km from center), in China; it was formerly called Lingang New City and renamed in 2012. Construction, which began in 2003, is designed to be completed in 2020. Aiming at half a million residents, the concept is to attract 10 million tourists a year. Still sparsely populated, it is expected to house more than 800,000 people.

Akin to the Korean example, the city design, as well as emerging from a swamp, is concentric to provide a focal hub, but, unfortunately in the Chinese case, the distances between buildings are so vast and the roads so wide that it is not a pedestrian but a vehicular city whose roads are built on the Beijing model, meaning there is no street life. As a future design model, it is seen as something to simply house an expanding population, but its character is difficult to see, and how Disney-styled theme parks will balance the otherwise dull nature of the rows of identical high-rise apartment buildings is unclear.

The big question that arises then is how to get people to live in such vast city complexes. This revolves around the chicken-or-egg question since, in the first instance, companies wish to locate wherever the action is, which, with few exceptions, isn't whether people are not, but at least in China, with its integrated planning, it can simply force people to relocate.[11] China can move people to match its planning, relocating government departments and educational facilities along with many government-owned businesses. The same applies to establishing learning institutions. In this case, there are eight universities lined up one after the

[10]L. Lin, and G. Ultrich. 2015. *Development of Smart Cities in China* (The Netherlands: Utrecht University).

[11]W. Shepherd. 2017. *Ghost Cities of China* (Boston, MA: Zeo Books).

other that will encompass an estimated 100,000 students. The reality is that whether individual persons like it or not, the government can simply mandate their location in this city. Overall, this is a very important issue in regard to future urban development, akin to "build it and they will come," even if forced to.

Smart Cities

A smart city is defined as a municipality that uses information and communication technologies to increase operational efficiency, share information with the public, and improve both the quality of government and services for citizen welfare.[12] This is possibly best demonstrated in reference to Barcelona, ranked among the front-runners in this field, with their concept of a three-stage process. The first of these is "top down" with technology-driven decision making incorporating smart open source data sensors and big data analytics into everything from parking and transportation to trash collection, air quality, and parkland irrigation.

In the second stage, "bottom up" takes over, where citizens and politicians drive the decision-making process. The third stage attempts to link the two with open access to the data bank for everyone, including politicians and commercial interests. A further innovation has been with "block city" concepts, in which areas are locked down and made vehicle free, enhancing other forms of mobility.

Other leading studies of smart cities rank Seoul (South Korea) first, followed by Vienna (Austria), Boston (the United States), Amsterdam (the Netherlands), Tokyo (Japan), Stockholm (Sweden), Paris (France), and then London and San Francisco.[13]

The basis for these ratings varies; in Seoul, in 2015, this was attributed to their health-care facilities, including innovations such as the provision of phones and tablets for sick people and hosting the upcoming 5G network. These cities will also supposedly be leading in the utilization of smart technology for mobility and transportation. Similarly, Vienna was

---

[12]Definition from www.whatis.com

[13]M. Luciano. November 2017. "Top 10 Smartest Cities in the World." www.ecnmag.com

renowned for its traffic management and was a leader in the use of green energy. Boston ranked first in governance, public management, and accumulation of human capital linked to universities such as Harvard and MIT. Amsterdam was first in governance and government digitization launching of incubator projects. Tokyo, then as the most populated city, was said to be the most tech savvy, also providing a reasonable blueprint of what cities will look like with a population of 15 billion. Stockholm was rated on greening and how its population recycles most of its waste. Paris and London were rated for their transport systems, with London and its business ecosystems. New York gets a mention in view of its link with Cisco Systems as lead developer of smart city concepts.

The real question becomes, what makes a city smart, and should this not be dependent on some happiness or welfare index or quality of life? Could this also then be linked with quality of housing along with its cost and how much of a person's life is taken up with earning an income simply to meet housing costs? The point raised here is illustrated by a reference from 2016 calculating how someone on an average salary would not be able to live in Beijing, the least affordable city along with Hong Kong and New York.[14] Sydney is well above London and Singapore in terms of cost of living, so where both husband and wife have to work to make ends meet, is this quality of life, and does it constitute living in a smart city?

If "happiness" is a basic indicator, on the assumption of humans being herd animals, living in close proximity to other people should provide some comfort, but it also implies some degree of personal interaction. The ability to instill some form of personal interaction within the structure of a city is therefore necessary to make a city smart.

Cluster Defensive

Following on from the concept of urban habitation for the future whose environment is designed for a specific few, guarded villages are not a new concept. In early times there were stockades, walls around the castles, and, in Africa, thorn bushes surrounding local villages. The defenses have long

---

[14]Centre for Inclusive Growth. July 2016. "How More Affordable Housing Can Impact Job Creation and Productivity."

been used against potential invasion and have also been favored in areas where high rates of crime prevail and where the topography allows them. That was the history of the past, and it still continues wherever necessary. Noteworthy here is that in each case there was a cluster of dwellings that needed to be protected.

Currently, clustered buildings continue to be protected in urban dwellings, either by fortifying individual houses or groups of houses or by building the concept into new residential developments when starting from an open space.

The guarded villages can have walls surrounding them, as in the Philippines, or demarcation signs, as in the United States, warning potential intruders. In some suburbs, such as in Johannesburg, in South Africa, if not villages, houses themselves are fortified. All have their own security services, and in countries like Kenya, or Tanzania, firms such as *Ultimate Security* provide panic buttons in houses and a guarantee to have armed response to a property within 6 minutes of an alarm.[15]

As to the hypothesis that in future the likelihood of disparity of wealth will increase, the extent of people wishing to live in a protected environment will also increase. In regard to habitats, this means that electronic response mechanisms will become commonplace so that attacks will at least be captured on CCTV footage somewhere, serving to discourage any intrusion. For long it has been argued that the poor do not need protection since they have nothing worth stealing. None of this, of course, can stop the occurrence of violence inside the home, but that is somewhat beyond the competence of urban planning.

Building Materials

Within the context of all of the above, the range of building materials to be used will vary greatly in relation to composition as well as method of construction. Already, it is possible to see building materials laser printed and laid down in various formats, utilizing many different types of material, including recycled waste.

---

[15]This is particularly important since the death penalty is awarded equally for armed robbery as for murder.

Demonstrations have circulated on laser printing of entire houses in a day, and many modular systems are available that, while modest in size, are fully functional, relatively inexpensive, readily mobile, and capable of being erected quickly. The limiting factor remains where to put them.

Other than solid structures, tents have been used to establish large-scale emergency housing and have a proven durability record. They can also be shipped at short notice anywhere in the world[16] as a short-term solution, although, unfortunately, this often turns into long term.

Further Urban Development Concepts

Social Cohesion

The answer to the question of what makes for a happy city from the world happiness index is healthy longevity followed by many definitions of required social interaction. This basically encompasses the facilities of the city and how they allow people to interact with and support one other. One part of this comes from what government support can provide, but the other focuses on group and family interaction.

Future planning needs to address this question of interaction, which becomes more difficult, with people locked onto their mobile phones even while in crowds, in restaurants, or on public transport. For future urban development, complexes will need to address the issue of constraints against isolation by providing facilities aimed at enforcing social interaction. Exactly how that is achieved is open for bright ideas in the future.

Local cafés or bars in housing complexes can act as meeting points, but, generally, people in these tend to keep to themselves, and while the local gyms allow for some interaction, people still rarely interact. Individuals appear to be more interested in connecting to people through their social media sites than in physically communicating, as can be seen when complete carriages on trains have everyone glued to their mobile devices. At present there does not appear to be a ready solution for bringing people

---

[16]Danish firm Vesterguard Franzen, whose head office is in Switzerland, has supplied planeloads of tents, blankets, buckets, and "life straws" to refugee camps from their large stores.

together other than through establishing special interest and sporting clubs. Online dating site success appears yet to be rated.

One way people used to be brought together was on cruise ships, which allowed time to get acquainted and to form relationships. This is made a little more difficult with the enormous cruise ships now operating, but the possibilities to connect still remain.

To mitigate isolation of individuals, some residential complexes aim to limit residents to specific age groups, providing facilities for young people who would want to live and party together and, at the other end of the spectrum, providing retirement villages offering group entertainment and sightseeing engagements.

Work-Oriented Clusters

Future urban development will involve clusters formed by urban spread as well as special-purpose clusters, as with Silicon Valley. The operational concept here will be to provide uncluttered linkages for people to move and exchange ideas between similar companies. This will involve work sites as well as the equivalent of dormitory accommodation.

The logical progression into the next hundred years will be toward elimination of private ownership of vehicles in favor of groups and along the lines of the Uber concept of web-based booking and payment, initially with drivers but later without. Connective routes will likely also go underground now that improved boring methods are available. These vehicle changes will also affect the need for parking and garages, but the work clusters are mainly intended to keep like-minded people together so as to be able to stimulate exchange of ideas.

While keeping people in proximity, when needing to connect further, means of travel will likely also change with the development of more mobile walkways, tubular connectivity both above and below ground, and more small-scale flying vehicles.

Pedestrian-Oriented Design

In view of the time taken to get from one place to another, and the ability to do much business online, future urban development will be directed toward cities where vehicles are not required and pedestrians take over.

As with smart cities, the concept yet to become fashionable was so that as in the latest in Korea, people could walk to work and eliminate cars all together. Within this context, private ownership of vehicles will likely disappear, to be replaced by share vehicles if and when needed or by the eventual driverless car that arrives as required.

Tourism Development Zones

Some countries have built cities simply to attract tourists and design them for that specific purpose. Yongyu-Muui, in the port city of Incheon, was conceived to attract 134 million tourists (mainly from China) at a cost of $275 billion, to be opened in 2030. This was to include all the usual hotels, malls, casinos, etc., along with a theme park, water park, Formula One race track, a concert hall, and a medical tourism "healing town." Looking ahead, one has to judge whether these facilities will be fully utilized in future.

Tourism can be guided either by natural geographic attractions such as beaches and mountains or even by remoteness as well as with reference to specific events, whether sporting or religious. Alternatively, attractions can be man-made, as with theme parks such as Disneyland.

One of the main problems with natural attractions is that these can be limited in size, for example, the length of a beach, or at an extreme, visits to the Wailing Wall or the Crips in Jerusalem. In developing tourist towns around attractions that might be crowded out, these need to be expanded into other nearby attractions to take the pressure off the main features (that is, 10 minutes to see the Eifel Tower. . . too crowded to go up any-way. . . take a "selfie". . . then move on to Disneyland). As for theme parks or tourist sporting concepts, these also need to be suitably located to cater to the large numbers required to make them financially viable.

In addition to straight tourism, an associated tourism concept is that of providing academic institutions rather than theme parks. In Australia, for example, government income from people wishing to come to study is surpassed only by that from mining.

Sponge City Approach

A sponge city has the ability, brought on through necessity, to mainstream its urban water management into development policy and designs. Since some cities cannot simply pump away flood risks that encroach on ever expanding urban developments, the concept of sponge cities, headed by China, aims to have 80 percent of urban areas reuse at least 70 percent of rainwater in 16 cities by 2020.

The concept seeks to reduce the scale of rainwater runoff by enhancing absorptive capacities and spreading this more evenly. The current showpiece for this is in China, specifically, Lingang model city in Shanghai's Pudong district, featuring rooftop gardens, scenic wetlands for rainwater storage, and permeable pavements to store excess runoff. Similar developments have taken place in Xianmen and Wuhan.

Future Development of Smart Technologies

While electronic adaptations have already been engaged in future cities such as having children with chipped bracelets in Songbo city, Korea (eventually likely to have children themselves chipped), these developments should see massive expansion in future. Some applications have not yet been conceived. Future facilities in these cities can allow, for example, hospital appointments to be organized through phones; there are already car parks that work on plate recognition, dispensing with the need for tickets, and facial recognition will eventually do away with the need for credit cards. Bus services in China[17] already use facial recognition systems, and law enforcement agencies in China tracked down a journalist within 6 minutes in an experimental trial in 2017.[18]

Some companies have chipped their employees so that this activates which door can be opened, provides access to different levels of data, and clocks employees on and off as they enter the building. It is logical that this system be extended to all companies and for government servants.

In the first instance, there will be the wiring of individuals and their connectivity to their habitat, which will be designed to respond to their preprogrammed requirements, from waking them up in the morning to cooking and cleaning while also preprogramming and adjusting their

---

[17]Yinchuan, which lies 552 miles west of Beijing, is one of China's 200 smart cities.

[18]A Chinese Village is Experimenting with over 1.3 billion People Logged into a Social Credit Scheme Where they are Rewarded or Penalized for their Actions Including Family Behavior, *The Times*, October 31, 2018.

daily activities. Some of these functions already exist and are available at various prices, but they will become more commonplace, as with other examples of new technology that emerge, are quickly copied, and become cheaper in due course. This individual-linked technology already extends to advising on booking medical and dental appointments, and Australia has just introduced an online system recording everyone's medical histories, which is expected to be available first to all doctors and hospitals. As with so many other databases that are advertised as secure and personal, such records will soon be available to other commercial interests such as insurance companies and potential employers.

From the individual's habitat and interconnectivity, a logical progression would be a "city cloud" of technology running all services over a specific area. An issue that will have major consequences will be the "1984 Syndrome," which, with everyone microchipped or logged into facial recognition, will govern every aspect of life. While this will bring with it greater personal security and time-saving benefits, it will also allow populations to be manipulated to their disadvantage. The only possible compensation here is that every new generation comes in on a new reference point and generally accepts the status quo that an earlier generation might have found reprehensible. The real question here is whether the possibility of a central government herding populations into its own desired directions is in the interest of individuals or is reminiscent of sheep being herded together for fleecing, or cows led in for milking. All of this increases the difficulty in the definition of SMART between living and existing.

CHAPTER 12

Financing

Overall

The basic financial equation for funding future urban development will be as it is already starting, geared to the *user-pays* principle. No matter how brilliant an urban development strategy is, it is of no use at all unless it can be financed. From an overall government perspective, there will never be sufficient money to do everything on a "wish list" to keep everyone happy. Consequently, there is a need to first work out clearly what a government might plan to include on its "wish list," test these aspirations against what best suits the target population, fit them within a political model and the prevailing legal system, and then look at how to fund it. One of the problems with the model is in the separation of planning from financing, which would be better served if there were closer integration between the two. That is, the planners plan but don't understand the financing needs, and the financiers are not included in the planning process. In some instances the laws will need to be changed to facilitate the planning model.[1]

With regard to the financing model, the majority of funding usually comes from government allocations out of general revenue in a democratic society based on political expediency to garnish votes, and is then supplemented on the user-pays principle on what can be taxed from local authorities, including rates and taxes, and then from specific taxes on everything from garbage collection to parking fees, roads, bridges, airport, on an endless list of things from which money can be extracted.

---

[1] With regard to centrally planned economies, in China anything can be done unless a specific law says it can't, while in Vietnam nothing can be done unless a specific law says it can.

To further ease the financial burden on government, the private sector is engaged to take over and run what might otherwise be public services, so they hand over ownership of facilities such as airports and harbors as well as power supply and garbage disposal. The model can extend on a "carrot versus stick," where apartments and whole cities can be constructed on land offered by the government if the investor will build. Thus have whole cities been built, as demonstrated in China and Korea. In Singapore, buildings have been erected on landfills created artificially utilizing processed and recycled waste where "water space" was made available.

In accepting the basic premise of "user pays" as akin to taxation, this principle is as old as the cavemen needing to give the biggest among them more food in exchange for protection (or for not being beaten). It explains how current planning evolves and shows how it is likely to continue in future.

Government Funding

The first part of this model of "user pays" is to identify the users. The simplest demonstration is where roads or bridges can be hit with tolls so users either have to use and pay or find some other route. Governments are ahead on that one, making access to alternatives unattractive, forcing vehicles onto the toll roads and leaving drivers unable to do anything about that.[2] That principle is even easier with bridges.

In reality, the user-pays model extends to almost everything in human existence and in being permitted to live.

People who live in houses can be taxed on their properties, and cars can be taxed, as can the basic amenities, power and water, food, and even entertainment. Then there is tax on any income. The ultimate catchall is value added (VAT) or sales tax, which government imposes on (almost)[3] every transaction. If there is anything not yet taxed, governments have departments to work on any loopholes, forever looking at ways and means

---

[2]In 2018, Vietnamese drivers responding to one toll judged unfair took to paying in small-denomination notes in protest, clogging up the system and forcing change.
[3]Small numbers of politically driven items, such as food, and, as in Australia recently, women's sanitary items, can be excluded.

of slipping in increases in tax, as quietly as possible and ensuring no tax is avoided.

The most current taxation development is through the electronic connectivity and data collection, where, in the first instance, government has access to individuals' bank accounts that are available to the tax or revenue departments. Try and use cash, and that is made more difficult in countries that have raised red flags where banks have to report cash deposits exceeding a certain amount.[4] It is also becoming almost impossible for the average person to work out how they are being charged for their power, water, Internet and phone bills, but VAT is added anyway. The fact that companies along with governments now specifically plan to make it difficult, if not impossible, to lodge complaints with a human, or in any event a human in your own country, makes people give up trying to complain and instead just pay their VAT bills and get on with their lives. The indication is that this apathy will continue into the future since the same IT that provides such valuable access to most information is also used to deny access to obtaining answers if companies or governments find this expedient.

Obviously, since individuals typically do not want to be taxed, people are always looking at ways and means of avoiding tax, which used to be relatively simple when individual countries used to have their own sovereignty, unlike now. Switzerland, for example, now has to supply bank details to the U.S. Revenue service on any American citizens holding Swiss accounts and with U.S.-derived income,[5] and even accounts in the Bahamas are under such tight scrutiny that this avoidance has become less helpful. In addition, many countries are working together to isolate tax avoiders and closing loopholes so as to collect as much tax as they can. Governments want as much money as possible so they can spend it on winning voter support.

Despite tightening the noose on tax avoidance and taxing anything they can find, most governments have a major funding problem owing to the size of investment expenditure required to handle major projects,

---

[4]A cash deposit limit of AU$10,000 was introduced in Australia in 2018, matching similar flagging for any import into the country.

[5]However, if you declared to the Swiss Bank that there was no United States–derived income, the Swiss Bank would believe you.

which could run not just beyond one project cycle but over more than one political stint in power. One government might try to plan a long-term development locking in the funding against the next government's wishes, but this does not help stability. Development projects also become political footballs, with promises made before elections by parties that have no way of backing their promises. On the other hand, authoritarian regimes are not hampered by these constraints.

While private sector funding is required to supplement what government cannot achieve on its own, other than in exceptional cases, government funds the major infrastructure and then allows the private sector to fill in. Examples would be with new road or rail developments leading to areas where the private sector can then fund the housing and shopping centers. The constraining issue remains the availability of jobs in new areas along with connectivity. In Sydney, Australia, the government, after 30 years of discussion, has finally agreed to a secondary airport at Badgerys's Creek, approximately 50 km west of Sydney. Jobs will need to be created nearby, but flying for, say, 20 hours from Europe, passengers would then have a ninety-minute bus trip into Sydney, as against landing in Sydney itself. Models like this work only if employment brings the people in, although speculators are the first to enter. This demonstrates the importance of building in connectivity with other larger urban centers. Centrally planned economies find it easier to allocate funds over longer periods and, as in the case of supercities, can simply build them and then direct people to live there.

Without a universal government deciding development plans, countries will continue to have different rates of development, constrained by the funds they have available and the political pressures they face. This fact determines how wealthier countries can benefit from the ability to fund trade routes, allowing their commerce to flourish, providing ports with modern handling systems, airports, and country-connective road and rail networks. China, as part of its trade development plans, is allocating billions of dollars to reopening the old trade route from its East Coast through to Europe.[6]

---

[6]Chinese OBOR (One Belt One Road) project earmarking $900 billion.

Part of the financial facilitation for developing countries will come from multilateral agencies such as the World Bank, Asian Development Bank, and the European Union, and through bilateral agencies such as Japan International Cooperation Agency (JICA), Department for International Development (DFID), and Danish International Development Agency (Danida). These are supplemented by nongovernment organizations (NGOs), which have to find their own funding either from the former or linked to charities or specific government-funded programs.

Apart from enhancing supply routes and value chains for product distribution, donors have trained their focus on *climate change* and *global warming*, the frightening yet emotive concept around which a wide range of planning initiatives are now focused. As these concepts attract large amounts of finance for reactive projects under an overall concept of *greening*, priority is given to the allocation of still limited funds. That is, under a climate-change-cum-greening concept they determine the most important aspects that should be funded first and the required level.

Particularly difficult are, for example, situations involving long time periods. Large-scale projects are spread over a span of many years, locking in funds that cannot then be used elsewhere.[7] Within the supply of this greening climate change aid, if seawater is washing away houses on a foreshore, are funds allocated for fixing the problem intended for all such houses countrywide or only for those with available money, and how does a planner decide which? How do slums get cleared while pressure is on for providing new housing? How about when people do not have clean water or treatment facilities for wastewater, which could be seeping into groundwater? Someone has to decide the allocation.

Overall, government is responsible for deciding on its own development plans and allocating money accordingly. Central to all of this is the political dimension, and in democracies, in particular, votes largely direct oil at the "squeaky wheel." Even in more authoritarian regimes, where the public might not be able to choose targets at which development expenditure is to be directed, they do have a limited ability to complain and so remain politically driven.

---

[7]Even China's OBOR proposed investment is so large and the returns so long term that it is at risk when the money is also required in the short term.

Governments then have the overall problem of allocating their limited resources and are in turn limited by their political life in that developments might expand beyond their tenure, and more voter support would be attracted if outlaid for current projects. Projects such as satellite cities, high-speed rail links, or regional airports would fall into this category. Future benefits have to be sold along with current benefits to justify the expenditure (or borrowing), such as by promising that the proposed development would ease current overcrowding and provide better connectivity and less time on the road. This remains difficult to do when people normally want to see short-term results.

The issue of borrowing becomes a major political issue for sovereign governments that raise funds against their promises to repay. Assuming the sovereign risk is secure for major countries such as the United States, they can continue borrowing, but this does not always work out, as evidenced by countries such as Argentina or Greece. Borrowed money still has the problem of having to win votes on long-term infrastructure projects, so one way governments get around this is to take the development off the books and "quarantine" it from annual expenditure. This disguises it from annual budgets, and the cost becomes less apparent.[8]

The problem here is that sovereign debt comes in many forms. The United States raises its own personal debts, but even individual states can borrow money for their own development on the assumption that their economies are wealthy enough to ensure that the money will be paid back; California, for instance, had a gross domestic product (GDP) of $2.75 trillion in 2018, more than that of the UK, at $2.62 trillion. It has a higher income than any other state and succeeds only the United States, as a whole, China, Japan, and Germany.[9] Technically, it could become bankrupt in its own right, but lenders would assume that the federal government would cover this.

If own funds are insufficient, governments and their planners need to explore, within the laws of the developing country concerned,

---

[8]The Australian National Broadband Network, requiring A$49 billion, was removed as a separate entity on the presumption that it would be self-funding and recoup the cost although with cost blowout is unlikely to happen.

[9]*USA Today* May 5, 2018.

supplementary sources of financing such as ODA, other agencies, development banks, or sovereign borrowing. The methods of raising supplementary finance will depend on the credit rating of a particular country.[10]

The bottom line, then, is that funding depends on the specific law of the country, enabling different levels of government to finance themselves and incur debt. In Vietnam, for example, only the five "supercities" are free to raise their own bonds, and the majority of other borrowing comes from special purpose units such as Local Development Infrastructure Funds (LDIFs).[11] The provincial governments do not do this directly, in view of the constraint in the country that nothing can be done unless a specific law specifies that it can, while in China anything can be done unless, as was noted earlier, there is a law saying it can't.[12] Consequently, China financed major development through urban development investment corporations (UDICs) that had to be curtailed, putting pressure on Treasury.

On the one hand is the concept of making the users pay balanced out on a long-term equation against those who may not be able to afford to pay. This then returns to the overall premise that future long-term planning will need to cater to everyone, not just those who can afford to pay for it. This therefore calls for a survey of the funding options.

Funding Equality

To make taxation seem equitable, it is usually directed to being higher for those who can most afford it, and this has a luxury tag. Hence, people who own property in the form of real estate or houses can be taxed simply for ownership and on its sale or transfer. People who own vehicles can be taxed and rates based on degree of luxury, while driving any form of vehicle can raise taxes on the required fuel.

---

[10]Led by international rating agencies that establish benchmarks defining lending levels, terms, and rates.

[11]Under Decree 138.

[12]An Australian funded project in 2000 was to auction off numerous nonperforming Vietnamese state-owned enterprises, but this was halted days before the auction on the grounds that no specific law allowed auctions. Meanwhile, China introduced a law in 2005 specifying that providing hostesses in business transactions was a bribe.

In taxing land as a ready source of funding, it is necessary to set a valuation base. This can be on commercial estimates, on land size, on land and buildings, which include location, or set according to an area average market price. The taxes can also be brought in by different agencies, so you can have local authorities (councils), state and central government taxes, or any combination. Introducing taxes for the first time can be problematic for political reasons but is usually done by governments keeping the rate low, excusing the poor by setting lower ceilings,[13] to raise them later when the principle has been accepted. In addition, the "bracket creep" comes in as earnings increase.[14]

The discussion on taxes raises the important question of ownership disparity, the situation in the United States being reflected by the following statistics: The richest 1 percent are said to hold about 38 percent of all privately held wealth, while the bottom 90 percent hold 73 percent of all debt.[15] Part of this disparity has evolved because of taxation methods that make it easy to tax wages earned, while people with money to invest have a multitude of legal ways to reduce their tax burden; this has been demonstrated even in movies showing how the so-called richest man in America did not himself own anything but did control it.[16] Then there is the newest model, by means of which Amazon looks to increase its value by driving up share price, not by paying dividends to increase wealth; the poor, however, are unlikely to be holding Amazon shares.

Looking to the future, the big question is going to be in relation to this linkage between the user and paying for what urban development requires if the predictions toward increased unemployment have any validity. As the leading minds of the generation, including Stephen Hawkins, have predicted, up to 60 or 80 percent of jobs will be lost in the foreseeable future because of artificial intelligence (AI) encroachment, therefore making it necessary to find ways to sustain this population who will still

---

[13]In Vietnam, no tax was proposed for any property under $39,000, but that would still tax 97 percent of the population.

[14]Tax rates increase as earnings increase, so government receives higher tax.

[15]New York Times, February 2017.

[16]J. Paul Getty portrayed in the movie *All the Money in the World,* Sony Pictures 2017.

be users but unable to pay for the use.[17] Hawkins reaffirmed this belief in a book released after his death.[18] Such a gap between those able to generate wealth and the basics of human existence, including provision of habitat, and the remaining vast numbers of people unable to contribute if this is the eventual outcome, will have enormous consequences in terms of social engineering. It will raise the question of standard of living right down to whether those with no wealth would be entitled to receive a share of wealth or, at the extreme, whether under social engineering they would simply be herded into camps to live in or just eliminated.

Official Development Assistance (ODA)

While individual countries will vary in their ability to provide the basic human habitat for their populations, the wealthier countries have long participated in funding the development aspirations of the less fortunate.[19] Consequently, developing countries can receive assistance for their infrastructure development through ODA, basing them on level of development. The least developed do not have to pay interest on their "borrowings," which kicks in as they emerge through different stages of development, having played by the dictated rules,[20] and they have loan durations of 30 or even 40 years, so repayments are less in current day prices when they fall due.[21] Hence, terms of funding vary by country, with the least developed receiving basically grants, while the next level up can obtain concessional funding at low rates of interest. The ODA is delivered through a multitude of so-called development banks such as

---

[17]See P. Nelson. 2018. *UBI and the Threat to Democracy as We Know It* (New York, NY: Business Expert Press).

[18]S. Hawkins. October 19, 2018. *Brief Answers to the Big Questions* (Seattle, WA: Amazon).

[19]One of the concepts was at the same time to provide sufficient local incentives to deflect migration.

[20]In a number of cases, undeveloped countries deemed unable to ever repay their loans have had them canceled.

[21]Depending on inflation rates, $1,000 today would be worth around $60 in 30 years' time. Stock Market 2013.

the World Bank,[22] Asian Development Bank,[23] and African Development Bank.[24] One problem with this model is that such low-cost finance comes with strings attached, requiring recipients to abide by what the donors determine are best for them, even if it does not always suit the best interests of the recipient.

ODA funding is technically underwritten as sovereign loans, but these are subject to strict implementation guidelines and reporting procedures. What can be funded must also comply with schedules of approved criteria, which currently focuses on *climate change and green growth,* and countries lacking basic services are hard put to show how they have a nice green central city park alongside slums. The unknown factor would be whether in a 100 years there would remain any least developed countries or whether the rest of the world would be both willing and in a position to carry on the assistance.[25]

While it is a delicate subject to cover, through the 1960s and 1970s and the assumed cold war between the United States and Russia (then it was the USSR), extensive competition prevailed between the two sides to win minds in Africa, which was eventually abandoned owing to financial constraints and the diminishing cold war rivalry. Meanwhile, in the last 20 years, China has moved into major countries in Africa, bringing with it considerable money offered for development projects that are seemingly untied and have few restrictions, although implemented with Chinese labor. A similar situation is emerging, that of Chinese infiltration through the Pacific, with only Tuvalu holding out in support of Taiwan for financial support. Consequently, while benefits are distributed to developing countries, strings of one kind or another are usually

---

[22]The International Bank for Reconstruction and Development, formed under the Bretton Woods Agreement for post–Second World War restructuring, continued on. It has always had an American president and has hence been able to align policy.

[23]Formed with initial funding by the Japanese to allow them to return to Asia after the Second World War. It has always had a Japanese president and has hence been able to align Japanese policy.

[24]IFAD, IFC, EIB, IsDB, EBRD, CAF, and others that can easily be identified.

[25]President Trump, in October 2018, announced cancellation of assistance on political grounds.

attached to aid, suggesting how this will be viewed in retrospect 100 years from now.[26]

Private Sector

Private sector participation in urban development is applicable in the context of both developing and developed countries. While major developments will usually be led by government, particularly in cases requiring land clearing and resettlement, private companies have in some cases undertaken to provide not just housing but also airports and ports, and in other cases, as in China and Korea, contracted to build and run whole cities.

In addition to taking part in the actual construction of facilities, the private sector can simply provide finance either directly or by underwriting bonds. Alternatively, groups can establish specific development companies and fund via IPOs,[27] which are intended to make a profit. The private sector development rule is that finance can be raised provided evidence can be furnished that funds are available, that it is assumed that funds are owned (or there is access to them, as in the Paul Getty case), if someone has a brilliant money-making idea (funding a startup such as Apple), or an investor has already spent money that they would lose unless they spent more.[28]

All of the foregoing might be old news. The big issue that needs to be considered for future development will be the impact of the inevitable supercompanies that will take center stage most likely within the next hundred years. There are already the giant companies, and while the most recognizable, Amazon and Google,[29] have developed new models designed not to make profits but to focus on shareholder price, it needs to be seen where the real money is. The biggest companies are in the car

---

[26]Many have argued that obsolete equipment was offloaded onto developing countries as aid, which in reality restricted development.

[27]Initial public offerings to premium investors.

[28]Trump case with his casino investment allowed to trade out on use of his name.

[29]Sinopec group, China National Petroleum, Toyota, Volkswagen, Royal Dutch Shell, Berkshire Hathaway, Exon Mobile, www.financeonline.com

and oil industries, which one might believe would put up some resistance to the removal of petrol-driven vehicles in future.

In regard to the question of size dominating and shaping things to come, the retail chains have already largely replaced the corner store beyond the convenience of 7-Elevens or their ilk, and this is likely to continue with the entry of these chains into a wide variety of industries such as insurance and banking, together with the ability to hold down prices on their supply chain. If one couples how this works alongside AI-induced job losses, the removal of small-size traders, the takeover of the primary producers, and a dominance across banking sectors, these conglomerates will be able to influence urban developments in a scenario where there is already a major department store and a McDonald's "in an area near you." Leaving aside the question of whether this is either good or bad, it is notable that governments are becoming more restricted in their planning and are losing some of their control.

The situation with these supercompanies and conglomerates is that they are already growing so large as to be able to distort the user-pays funding model, in that, as noted earlier in reference to Amazon and similar other companies, by running without profits to be taxed and relying on wealth creation through share price increase, they put governments at a considerable disadvantage. There is also the overall question, beyond what has been discussed here, of possible major job losses in future that will likely reduce the income tax base further distorting the user-pays model.[30]

The question overall is whether the future will be driven by super-wealthy conglomerates or whether governments will retain power under an economic system, and in the longer term whether this will bring about a change in the way governments can organize urban planning. With this comes the question of the possible interaction of such supercompanies and their need to eventually support a population with unemployment predicted at 60 to 80 percent. This might lead to governments having to pay the majority of the public welfare and the "supercompanies" being the only ones earning enough to provide the finance.

---

[30]P. Nelson. 2018. *UBI and the Threat to Democracy as We Know It*, op.cit.

Packaging

Looking at funding an urban development strategy, from the smallest initiative to the largest complex project, it is fairly obvious that merely laying out a plan is not sufficient unless the government has the financial capability to package the required funding to make implementation possible.

If, as hypothesized earlier, the superconglomerates come to assume an integral part of future planning, the question arises as to whether they will become "benevolent dictators" or use their power to dictate their own objectives? Here it has to be remembered that in the case of retailers, these stores already have an incredible volume of personal information, often linked to individuals' loyalty cards so that they are already able to influence shopping habits, and it can only be assumed that such ability will be increased enormously in times to come. They can not only manipulate their customer base with loyalty cards but also squeeze their suppliers who have no other market outlet. Already, they use store positioning to drive down prices.

In offering a defense, one of the excuses emerging from the recent Australian Banking Royal Commission was that the banks were only working in the interests of their shareholders and, while having certain legal requirements, were ruled not to be under any obligation to be benevolent. The same would apply to these conglomerates. While bad publicity might dissuade certain customers, it has been found that shoppers are for a short time price sensitive rather than morally dissuaded.

The question that arises is, where within government's planning departments are the experts who can carry forward the overall development concepts, and are these departments actually a match for these monolithic corporations of the future? It is no simple matter for government to be able to simply lay out an urban plan, assuming it had all the finance, and proceed to implement it, for, given the recognition that demand always exceeds supply, it will rarely be able to do this on its own and will need to package its funding. China can do this by ordering companies to comply with what they want or face the consequences, whereas in democratic societies such compliance will not be forthcoming without some financial incentive.

An example of the financial *packaging* required would be where the government would like to drain a swamp and turn it into a park.[31] Someone comes to them with a proposal to build a nearby mall. They are told that they can have their mall if they also fix the swamp or that the city needs affordable housing within a developing context. The developer who wants land and approval for his 40-storied apartment development is told, "Yes but build shops on the ground level, parking underground, low-cost apartments for the first six floors,[32] no lift required, and then make your profit on the next floors up." Do that and you get your approval. The question will be whether governments have sufficient power to implement such a packaging system or whether civil servants in the planning departments have the knowledge and skills to handle such negotiations with developers.

Consequently, there needs to be legislation within government allowing this sort of commercial negotiation and packaging to take place, and within that, it requires suitably trained and experienced people to carry out the task. Crucial to all of this, from a future perspective, will be the development of AI and, in the longer term, the question of who wields control—the government or the business conglomerate—since it's unlikely to be the user.

---

[31] The Korean future green city, Songdo, was built on reclaimed swamp.

[32] Fitting in, for example, with laws providing no life required up to six floors.

CHAPTER 13

Enforcement

Theory

Under the theory of separation of powers in a democracy, the government legislates and establishes the laws, whereas a separate body interprets and issues penalties for violations. Obviously, no system is perfect, and while there is a separation, the judges under the second wing are nevertheless appointed by the first wing; hence the government is unofficially beholden to them for the appointments. It is also difficult to see that an absolutely fair outcome is achieved when a panel of judges does not reach a unanimous decision but that is the best there is said to be available.

In planning theory, the planners within government set out what they feel are best practices; these are put into a legal framework and are then expected to be followed. As with all development, money can be involved and shortcuts to the regulations could save millions if the law can be bypassed without redress. Such a situation puts immense pressure on the legal system and on those designated to implement the decisions. It is also unrealistic to have effective enforcement when the same government making the rules is also the enforcer. No amount of monetary penalty is really a deterrent when it comes out of the same budget.

Practice

One of the difficulties in enforcement comes from this reality of government being both the planner and the enforcer. Especially in the context of a least developed country, where the overall aim is improvement of GDP, a development is unlikely to be curtailed because of some environmental law. In developed countries, the separation in the law makes it less likely that violations in planning laws would go unnoticed, but with the considerable amount of money that could be involved there have been many cases where corruption has taken place. One could only speculate on the reason why so many real estate developers have links to local councils.

Specifically, in developing countries, if someone comes along and says they will fund major development that would help advance the careers of local officials, the people at the top are unlikely to be overridden by the lowly planners at the bottom, and regulations could simply be changed or just overlooked.[1] It is also easier to hide kickbacks in less developed economies and to distract journalists from following up stories at the risk of imprisonment or worse. Add to this the ability to rationalize where companies in first world countries employ agents in third world ones who pay the bribes that are then billed as various legally permissible expenses.

Against this generalization over what happens in practice with particular reference to underdeveloped economies, there was the recent instance mentioned on Boracay, in the Philippines, where this pristine leading holiday island resort became overwhelmed by tourism, and a flurry of unrestrained building of houses and hotels, along with the pollution, was created. The local mayor simply closed down the entire island and issued notices for noncompliant buildings to be altered or, in some cases, completely demolished. Action here had to be taken since the problem became too visible. The island, as mentioned, was reopened to tourists in October 2018, but the question was really whether this action would have been taken had the island's fame not guaranteed that tourists would return. There had not previously been a total shutdown of Puerto Galera.

Monitoring

To overcome the problem of development driving infrastructure expansion beyond the constraints of containing legislation within government policy overriding the latter, the best way around this is through public monitoring. Where governments know that their execution of policies will be subject to public scrutiny, or, as in Boracay, when this pollution

---

[1]The Barangaroo Casino development, in Sydney, changed all the rules to support a major expansion.

story hit the international media, they are more likely to pay attention to environmental legislation.

Having suggested public disgracing as a control mechanism, there are some countries that have even had front-page headlines on how planning policies have been ignored without the slightest reaction from government.[2] No action was taken against anyone. In one instance $250 million disappeared on a project, and the two men involved are free, while the journalist who printed the story is in jail.

Fake News

Unfortunately, the question of fake news cannot be ignored now that it has become a mainstream issue emerging from the recent election of Donald Trump and assertions of Russian and Chinese election interference. This is not that fake news has not been around since the earth was believed to be flat, but the reality around what people in fact want or don't want to see has become so clouded that it is hard to determine what is real. This is exacerbated by the fact that almost anyone can download free source software that can clone people in videos not just on photos, and investigative journalism has become a casualty of online sensationalized private reporting.

Even when real issues are reported on, they come forward at such a rate that no one has the time or the inclination to follow anything up before the next story comes along. Thus do issues of corruption, at even the very highest level, pass quickly by, and stories move on to the next allegation, leaving people unable to defend themselves. The outcome is that more and more real criminal activities, let alone planning violations, can go under the radar, regardless of the legislation, as authorities simply don't have the time to pursue all allegations.

Political organizations can now require access to people's social media as well as phone listings to carry out millions of Robo calls to push their agendas, whether this is by fake opinion polls or fake allegations against politicians or their policies. The methods currently used are fairly sophisticated, calling into question their authenticity and, in any event,

---

[2]Vietnam Daily News front-page headline September 22, 2017.

to an individual's inability to respond. This spread of fake news or "robo calling" is repeatedly carried out on the eve of an election, and while astute Internet users are becoming more accustomed to sifting through the propaganda, the sheer volume of the fake material circulated will have some effect.

In regard to the legal framework concerning dissemination of fake news, laws have been passed in some jurisdictions on cyberbullying, but this becomes extremely difficult in the political sphere since, for some reason, defamation does not extend to that space, nor is it easy to trace originators of fake news, and even if it were possible, irreversible damage would usually be done before legal action could be taken. Hence, the really serious issue in regard to fake news is that the damage disseminated goes beyond what can be handled by due legal process, which appears to be lagging a long way behind. Former prime minister of Australia Bob Hawke was famous for taking out injunctions against anyone who said anything bad about him until the news died down and he withdrew the actions, but under the present system, the damage would have been done before he had the chance to take out the injunctions.

Penalties

Penalties for building violations have to be appropriate to the extent of the breach; otherwise they have no meaning. Action needs to be shown to have been taken and followed through despite the conflicting issues arising through fake news. A problem in developing countries is that one side of government identifies the culprits, and another then extracts bribes.[3]

Penalties can involve a fine, rectification of a construction, such as recent experience with the fire-prone cladding outside buildings, and total removal of the structure or jail time.

In a developing country context, it is unlikely that any penalty would usually require a building to be torn down,[4] and with the disparity in

---

[3]In one East African country, a project identified tax dodgers. No official action was taken against the wealthy Indians involved, but money was then extorted from them according to involved eyewitnesses.

[4]Except in the Philippines, on Boracay Island, on a recent case in 2018, where the author owned property and had firsthand experience.

income, underhand payments are an easy way around regulations. Through this even when building codes have been ignored or bypassed, wealthy developers confined to simple to get governments to introduce new regulations approving what they've ready constructed. In this way, major violations can go unpunished, while the poor man can have his tin shed pulled down. Add to this the fact that most civil servants are afforded protection for their activities, while the politicians responsible rarely fall on their swords.

On the other hand, people in China and Bangladesh have been jailed, if not executed, for building violations leading to deaths in building collapses. Both of those countries are also on record for jailing owners of substandard buildings that had collapsed, but whether the culprits remained in jail is difficult to prove.

CHAPTER 14

Political Ramifications

Considering that this analysis is aimed at projecting what policy decisions might look like when planned from a 2120 perspective, the critical overall issue will finally depend on global political structures. The bottom line will be whether the majority of the world's population will accept the global political map of the day, whatever that will be, or whether circumstances dictate that enough people will have the willingness, influence, and power to move against the status quo.

Current Political Dominance

A geopolitical map would show that the United States currently has economic dominance, followed by China, which is fast emerging. The European Union as a group, backed by the North Atlantic Treaty Organization (NATO), would be the third dominant group, but their political power is distributed between many countries, and now, with BREXIT, has been diminished further. Russia, in that mix, is also attempting to reemerge and reexert its influence in the Middle East, as reflected by the situation in Syria. It's not just where these groups are positioned now but the speed at which changes are occurring.

This has relevance to planning for the future of urban development; specifically, the course along which the political situation evolves has major implications for who will survive better and how living conditions will be organized in future. This includes the interaction between the developed and the undeveloped and the rich and the poor and the manner in which the balance of wealth will be adjusted in years to come. There are innumerable factors governing this, including how countries will be ruled and whether the sheer numbers of a disadvantaged class will simply accept their lot or have the will or capacity to do anything about it if they do not.

A further factor that has influenced most past global political shifts has been internal unrest. Driven by the sheer number of inhabitants on the planet needing to find a living, such divisions are rising, and their consequences could lead to major political shifts in the future.

Uprising

A look at recent developments in the United States reveals how the political divide has become increasingly aggressive, with some sections resorting to violence in their protests. While this, of course, is happening in other countries as well, the United States can be seen taking the lead owing to its prominence on the world stage.

The question becomes whether the majority of people will stick by the imposed so-called democratic rules, depending on how one defines democracy, since the Electoral College in the United States shows that individuals are not elected on the basis of one person one vote,[1] or whether these disaffected groups will attempt to do anything outside the political process. It has to be remembered that America was founded upon revolution and by ousting their then legal British government, so, as with the Second Amendment and the right to bear arms, many Americans believe that they always have the right to overthrow the rule of law where it is deemed necessary. While this would seem a big call when considering an overthrow of the military, the general dissatisfaction can affect voting patterns. This could be manifest in the election of a president who is totally outside the political establishment and who decides to carry forward this revolution for the disaffected.

Currently, this American position is further complicated by communication channels where existing legal systems can be corrupted through the electronic media, enabling ghost voters to be included and other countries having the ability to manipulate outcomes by adjusting both real and fake news. The importance of this is that, given the volume of news coming out on a daily basis, it is possible to release a global news story affecting a political situation that leaves no time for a response

---

[1] The Electoral College in the United States as agreed to on Federation attempts to balance the votes of states against individual votes.

declaring a story fake before the next story breaks. The corollary to this is that anyone can now do something for real, while protesting that it is not them becomes a believable defense.[2]

Should there be some form of uprising in leading countries such as America, where the majority of the population don't like the current system, the problem then becomes one of identifying what exactly those people want to replace it with.

At the same time in China, while any unrest against the dominant political system is not publicized, and while any that is can be held from the media, most of the internationally reported confrontations have come only from the non-Han, Muslim Uyghur[3]–based population in the northwest. Overall, however, despite China having its own planning problems in regard to disparity of incomes, it seems unlikely that a government overthrow will take place in the foreseeable future, especially when the bulk of the population see themselves in an ethnic ascendancy.

It should be remembered that Chinese people have a history of going along with what their rulers tell them to do, having seen demonstrations of the consequences of objecting, and while there is always a minority of dissent, the majority have demonstrated that they just go along with the party line and believe this is quite normal.

War

History shows that an attempt to change political systems generally leads to war. With the disruption in America between the Democrats and the Republicans becoming more violent and the historical acceptance of the right to overthrow the lawful government, it is unlikely that there will ever be a further civil war in which two established armies oppose each other, but other serious divisions could result.

Against the unrest in America is the ascendance of China, which, while having its own internal problems and social unrest, is able to control its population through both propaganda and physical restraint.

[2]Many websites contain compromising pictures of celebrities that are not real.
[3]They are one of 55 recognized ethnic minorities, living in Xinjang Autonomous Region of NW China.

The question becomes whether the differences between countries could lead to open conflict. In this mix comes Russia, which has lost most of its muscle following the demise of the Union of Soviet Socialist Republics (USSR) but remains in the equation in its bid to really assert itself by making things difficult for the United States.

The overall balance between the U.S.–Chinese aspirations is unlikely to lead to an all-out war, because, seen from the Chinese side, they have learnt how to get what they want by slow infiltration without overall aggression. An all-out war does not make economic sense, while, as can be seen by their emergence into the South China Sea, seeking strategic bases in other parts of the world achieves far better penetration. The main unknown in this equation holding them in check appears to be the wild card of not knowing the stability of President Trump and whether, on a bad day, some Chinese action could prompt an all-out confrontation. Trump has been successful in playing that bluff, but just as unpredictable are the Chinese, who, should they feel their hurt pride required a reaction, could spark an all-out war.[4]

It needs to be remembered that the focus of our discussion is the situation as it is projected to be in 100 years and that no political evaluation of the current period is being undertaken here. In relation to 2120, therefore, it can only be surmised that while all-out war between America and China aiming for global dominance will be unlikely to eventuate, there are likely to be serious regional skirmishes that will affect the balance of power.

A Global Political System

If it is likely that there will be no all-out war but only small-scale confrontations, then we can, on the basis of what is happening in America and the start of disintegration within the EU, expect that the next hundred years will see some political rearrangements, given that countries are less likely to operate independently and without considering the system as a whole.

---

[4]This is reminiscent of Chairman Mao's famous retort to the threat of war, namely, that China could lose 100 million and still win.

Attempting to come up with a world-style parliament, history has given the world the United Nations, which was intended to provide such a forum but produced a dysfunctional model instead. The system was intended to put all countries on a level playing field by giving each an equal vote, while at the same time removing the question of equality by having an inner Security Council of only the dominant nations with a mechanism allowing for policy decisions by the select few to be vetoed. The functionality is further reduced by the system of voting for the chief executive in the Secretary General, which in itself becomes highly political on the basis of one country one vote.[5] In an attempt to further the picture of equality,[6] there has been arbitrary rotation of membership of the Security Council, as in the selection of the Secretary General. Not that these selected men were not exemplary in their own right, but in this seeming lottery to fairness it becomes a question of inability to achieve anything if someone from Kuwait or Kazakhstan were appointed by the Security Council to chair committees on alleged terrorism involving, say, Iran.[7]

Adding to the constraints under the UN political model is the problem with the power to veto any proposed decision, which then becomes impossible to enforce. Here, the UN has often demonstrated that it is a toothless tiger. Any proposed general sanctions can simply be voted down on this basis of one country one vote, even when such countries contribute little funding and everything is in fact controlled by the permanent members of the Security Council. Even where sanctions are proposed against a Security Council member, they can be ignored. The main argument in favor of the UN has been that at least it provides a forum for discussion.

Notwithstanding the above, during the Obama reign and covered in his farewell speech, the UN unveiled its 2030 Agenda for Sustainable Development introducing a "new universal agenda for all mankind" (forgot to be politically correct and include women), aiming at making the UN a

---

[5]The tiny island of Tuvalu supports Taiwan with its vote.

[6]With, for example, past presidents such as Kofi Annan, of Ghana, and Javier Perez, of Peru.

[7]Counter Terrorism Committee chairs respectively from Kuwait and Kazakhstan. Security Council, July 13, 2018.

world government.[8] The plan bypasses the U.S. Congress and legislators of the other 193 nations. While again the concept of sustainable development behind the idea is commendable, given the track record of the UN to date, the idea of the UN deciding global issues outside and overriding the authority of national governments is far from logical.

It is hard to see how the existing system would allow any substantial changes to the UN structure as everyone would want more power. On the other hand, anything could happen should Trump decide that America will withdraw its payments or pull out of the UN. That would make it unlikely that the remaining members would be able to agree on a revised formula, with the likely outcome being that dominant countries would form their supreme planning authorities to administer their will and hand out largesse to win favor with poorer nations.

Acceptance

Since this text looks at decisions that might be made by those people who will be around a hundred years from now, encompassing all the possible changes in the meantime, the important issue will really be whether the global population has been conditioned or controlled into accepting anything decided by whatever form of government emerges. The first part of that equation is whether there will be several offsetting major governments in control or whether one country will meanwhile have emerged supreme. Alongside this, will there remain renegade "tribes" not prepared to accept the world order?

What appears to be certain is that governments or those in control will be further able to monitor people's existence along with everything about them, including their DNA and genetic codes. The implication of this is, of course, enormous since, as evidence is already emerging, it will be possible to determine individual likes from food that is eaten, who is desirable as a mate, the desirable genetic engineering of offspring, right through to voting preferences and how to put selections into office. The problem here, but outlined in many sci-fi movies, is that this data will not only be accessible by governments or rebellious movements, but also

[8]Adopted by UN Sustainable Development Summit, September 25, 2015.

usable for commercial purposes in that individual behavior can basically direct and manipulate to control wealth. These new systems on the way will be able to reduce free will and dictate what people should eat, whom they should mix with, their political beliefs and voting patterns, what is truth, what is not, and in other ways direct how people think. In all of this one needs to return to the cost factor and to recognize that in social engineering it becomes important, when there is the ability, to determine the exact cost to society of keeping a specific individual alive and how this fits into the overall economic equation. All of this then returns to the question of whether 100 years ahead society, faced with the controls possible on human behavior, will simply accept what they are told or whether there will remain some semblance of free thought? In regard to urban development, this means facing the situation of whether people have free choice on where and how they live, or whether they are simply told that this is the most expedient method of living and the population accepts this as inevitable, or normal.

CHAPTER 15

Planet Earth

What Is Known

With an ever-increasing population and greater connectivity, it is possible to view earth as a relatively ever-diminishing sphere in which all living creatures will still need to coexist. Ultimate survival depends on planning for humans' future, in which room has to be made for the survival of other animal species, if for no other reason than that any extinction of any life forms could be a forerunner to what happens to humans.

The question becomes of priority in survival be directed? The eight millennium goals of 2000, representing the best that countries could come up with at the time, may be a start but might also be seen as slightly ad hoc and, in light of the present, would need to be revised, so, for example, fixing extreme poverty and hunger should be preceded by the right to survive within a justifiable rule of law. Universal primary education may cover understanding of the required law, and there is no argument against gender equality and how all people should at least be permitted to be equal.[1] Then there is the far reaching, hard to define ensuring environmental stability to be achieved and the need to develop global partnerships for development. Eradication of major diseases should be a priority along with the capability to handle any new threats that might yet arise. There are identifiable fairly certain trends to which urban development will need to be directed such as the following:

- Populations and density of urban settlements in the absence of a catastrophe will continue to increase.

---

[1]Nelson, Peter 2018. *UBI and the Threat to Democracy as We Know It* (New York, NY: Business Expert Press). Postulates that men may eventually become superfluous and women could easily take over the world along with artificial intelligence (AI).

- Individuals overall will inhabit smaller self-contained and wired living spaces.
- Constraints on food and water will increase.
- People will continue to become obese owing to poor dietary habits and lack of exercise.
- The entire concept and delivery of education will change.
- Jobs will be lost, raising unemployment, and the one-job-for-life concept will cease to exist.
- The predominance of AI and connectivity with robotics will increase.
- The disparity in wealth and related income will increase.
- Individuals will spend more time on their interconnectivity via current devices and the yet to be invented communication media of the future.

What Is Unknown

Overall, the unknown depends largely on human reaction to the known.

- Will ethnic and religious divisions drive societies apart, or will proximity of cohabitation bring them closer together?
- Will religious beliefs be supplanted by scientific discovery?
- Will there be a move by governments to try to equalize people to reduce them to the lowest common denominator?
- What changes will there be in global geopolitical structures, and will these be balanced or usurped by one authoritarian regime?
- Will a central authoritarian regime determine how populations will live, and enforce compliance?
- Will populations through interconnectivity with AI become dissociated from reality?
- Will AI and robots take over most of the jobs on the planet, leaving humans to find other activities during their time on it?
- Will some biological or space-induced catastrophe destroy humanity?

Is the Best Yet to Come?

Considering that man's time span on the planet to date has been short, within the vastness of the universe, and the extent to which humans' understanding of science and technology has developed within that tiny period, it is impossible to know what the future might bring. The main point in what could be exciting times ahead suggests interfacing with other planets and intelligent life forms. What, in the meantime, needs to be ensured is that the current inhabitants of the planet look after their habitat so that they will continue to exist to experience the possibility of exciting things to come. Certainly, that generation experiencing 2120 will live in interesting times.

About the Author

Peter Nelson is an Australian economist and accountant who has operated his own chartered accounting and consulting company for over 30 years. He has worked on numerous assignments for a number of governments and for all major donors covering 52 countries, having also run the EU's largest project across China. His specialty has been on economic restructuring in its many forms, now attempting to look to the future and what that might bring. In his spare time, and aligned with business interests, he has been an avid scuba diver and raced his yacht internationally.

Index

OTHER TITLES FROM THE ECONOMICS AND PUBLIC POLICY COLLECTION

Philip Romero, The University of Oregon and
Jeffrey Edwards, North Carolina A&T State University, *Editors*

- *A Primer on Microeconomics, Second Edition, Volume II: Competition and Constraints*
  by Thomas M. Beveridge
- *A Primer on Microeconomics, Second Edition, Volume I: Fundamentals of Exchange*
  by Thomas M. Beveridge
- *A Primer on Macroeconomics, Second Edition, Volume II: Policies and Perspectives*
  by Thomas M. Beveridge
- *A Primer on Macroeconomics, Second Edition, Volume I: Elements and Principles*
  by Thomas M. Beveridge
- *Macroeconomics, Second Edition, Volume I* by David G. Tuerck
- *Macroeconomics, Second Edition, Volume II* by David G. Tuerck
- *Economic Renaissance In the Age of Artificial Intelligence* by Apek Mulay
- *Disaster Risk Management: Case Studies in South Asian Countries*
  by Huong Ha, R. Lalitha S. Fernando, and Sanjeev Kumar Mahajan
- *The Option Strategy Desk Reference: An Essential Reference for Option Traders*
  by Russell A. Stultz
- *Disaster Risk Management in Agriculture: Case Studies in South Asian Countries*
  by Huong Ha, Lalitha S. Fernando and Sanjeev Kumar Mahajan
- *Foreign Direct Investment* by Leena Kaushal

Announcing the Business Expert Press Digital Library

Concise e-books business students need for classroom and research

This book can also be purchased in an e-book collection by your library as

- *a one-time purchase,*
- *that is owned forever,*
- *allows for simultaneous readers,*
- *has no restrictions on printing, and*
- *can be downloaded as PDFs from within the library community.*

Our digital library collections are a great solution to beat the rising cost of textbooks. E-books can be loaded into their course management systems or onto students' e-book readers. The **Business Expert Press** digital libraries are very affordable, with no obligation to buy in future years. For more information, please visit **www.businessexpertpress.com/librarians**. To set up a trial in the United States, please email **sales@businessexpertpress.com**.

www.ingramcontent.com/pod-product-compliance
Lightning Source LLC
Chambersburg PA
CBHW061322220326
41599CB00026B/4990